William Hayden

An Introduction To The Study Of The Irish Language based upon

the preface to Donlevy's Catechism

William Hayden

An Introduction To The Study Of The Irish Language based upon the preface to Donlevy's Catechism

ISBN/EAN: 9783741175794

Manufactured in Europe, USA, Canada, Australia, Japa

Cover: Foto ©Andreas Hilbeck / pixelio.de

Manufactured and distributed by brebook publishing software
(www.brebook.com)

William Hayden

An Introduction To The Study Of The Irish Language based upon

the preface to Donlevy's Catechism

AN INTRODUCTION

TO THE

STUDY OF THE IRISH LANGUAGE

BASED UPON THE PREFACE

TO

DONLEVY'S CATECHISM

BY

REV. WILLIAM HAYDEN, S.J.

TEXT, TRANSLATION, AND GLOSSARY

DUBLIN: M. H. GILL, AND SON
LONDON: DAVID NUTT

EDITOR'S PREFACE.

THE following work has been edited for the purpose of supplying, in a small compass, and
for a small sum, all that is necessary for mastering
the elements of the Irish language. The only books
which the Editor considers necessary as companions
to the present work are the Second Irish Book and
Dr. Joyce's Grammar (Dublin: Gill & Son). Thus
for a few shillings anyone may furnish himself with
all that is necessary for learning Irish.

The Editor does not recommend to beginners the
use of a dictionary—for two reasons, one of which is
practical, and the other scientific. The practical
reason is founded on the fact that good dictionaries
are almost inaccessible. The most valuable works
on the Irish language have been allowed to fall out
of print. The few copies of such works that remain
in the country are rapidly disappearing from it,
being purchased at high prices by dealers, and by

our American brethren, who import into America every year large quantities of Irish books. If anyone has misgivings as to these statements let him inquire at the second-hand book-stalls of Dublin the price of Foley, Coneys, O'Brien, Donlevy, Neilson, &c.: he will usually find that the works are not to be had, and if they are to be had the price will be prohibitive.

The second reason for permitting the student to dispense with the use of a dictionary is that it is apt to divert the mind of the learner from the close study of the text. In learning Latin, Greek, or any strange language, the text should be, for the time being, the chief source of light to the student. By devoting himself almost exclusively to it he will arrive at a knowledge of the spirit and structure of the language —a knowledge never to be gained from the pages of a dictionary, which from the nature of the case will represent words, in their unattached state, drawn, with more or less judgment, from divers sources, and from different chronological periods of the language.

Donlevy is regarded by scholars as one of the most correct writers of modern Irish. The Glossary and Notes of the present work will furnish the reader with all that is necessary for mastering the text.

The present work will be useful to two classes of persons : first, to those who having no knowledge of Irish desire to acquire it; secondly, to that large class of persons who constitute a standing proof of the neglected state of education in this country, namely, persons who have a colloquial knowledge of Irish, but who are utterly unacquainted with its structure and grammar.

It may not be out of place to say that the student should endeavour to understand each section by the help of the adjoined translation, and of the Glossary. When he has made himself familiar with the meaning of the section he should endeavour to put the English into Irish, in writing if possible, but at all events in speech. If he does this several times he will find that his translation will gradually approximate to the text of the author, and the degree in which it does so will serve to gauge his own progress in the tongue he is learning. It is the want of some such method as this that explains a fact more frequently deplored than remedied by those who are interested in education. A boy may be engaged in learning Latin for four or five years; he may read considerable portions of Cornelius Nepos, Cæsar, and Cicero; yet at the end of the time he may be unable to translate an unseen passage from a Latin author, or to put a

simple English sentence into Latin. This bad state
of things, connoting as it does loss of time to the boy
and loss of money to his parents, arises from the fact
that he has been employed in passing, or endeavour-
ing to pass, from the unknown to the known, from
the Latin to the English. Had he mainly relied
upon the order which reason and sound logic recommend, the transition from the known to the unknown,
from the English to the Latin, he would be possessed
of a copious vocabulary, and would be himself an
accurate and fluent Latin speaker or writer.

In editing the text I have relied solely on the
Paris Edition of 1742. Donlevy had the advantage,
denied to the great Keating, of revising his work for
the press, and seeing it printed. In the opinion of
the present writer subsequent editions have fallen
short of the original edition, which bears upon it
every mark of conscientious carefulness and scholar-
ship. I have ventured on no alterations either in the
English or Irish, except that in many cases I have
introduced a hyphen in deference to modern usage,
and that I have often changed capital into small
letters.

For the benefit of readers who may not have an
opportunity of consulting the Paris Edition of 1742,
I shall here transcribe a passage from Donlevy on

the learning of the Irish language. It is taken from the Appendix. He is speaking of certain grammatical abuses which crept into the English language about the reign of King Charles II., and he thus proceeds :—

" It is no Wonder then, seeing the English Tongue, although in the Opinion of all, it be otherwise much improved, is thus maimed and confounded, even in Prose, that a Language (*i.e.* the Irish Language) of neither Court, nor City, nor Bar, nor Business, ever since the Beginning of King James the First's reign, should have suffered vast Alterations and Corruptions ; and be now on the Brink of utter Decay, as it really is, to the great Dishonour and Shame of the Natives, who shall always pass every where for Irish-Men : Although Irish-Men without Irish is an Incongruity and a great Bull. Besides, the Irish-Language is undeniably a very Ancient Mother-Language, and one of the smoothest in Europe, no Way abounding with Monosyllables, nor clogged with rugged Consonants, which make a harsh Sound, that grates upon the Ear. And there is still extant a great Number of old valuable Irish Manuscripts both in publick and private Hands, which would, if transcribed and published, give great Light into the Antiquities of the Country, and furnish some able Pen with Materials enough, to write a compleat History of the Kingdom : What a Discredit then must it be to the whole Nation,

to let such a Language go to Wrack, and to give no Encouragement, not even the Necessaries of Life, to some of the Few, who still remain, and are capable to rescue those venerable Monuments of Antiquity from the profound Obscurity they are buried in?"

The evil which Donlevy deplores in these last words has been to some extent remedied in a manner which he could never have anticipated. The scholars of Germany, France, and England, and the learned professor of Sanscrit in Trinity College, Dublin, are busy in working upon Irish manuscripts. It is to be earnestly desired that the aforesaid scholars may persevere and prosper in their noble task of rescuing the historical monuments of an ancient race from oblivion and contempt, and in thus providing a sure basis for historical studies.

WILLIAM HAYDEN, S.J.

Milltown Park, Dublin,
March, 1891.

ꝼoꝛꝼhóꝫꝛa.

I. 1 Cuıꝛꝼıḋ, do ꝛéıꝛ ċoꝛaṁlaċta, toıꝛt an teaꝫaıꝛꞡ
Chꝛíoꝛouıże-ꝛe, aıꝛ an ꝫ-ceuo aṁaꝛc, cꝛıoċnuꝫaḋ
aıꝛ an oꝛeam oo ċleaċt aṁáın ꝫeıꝛꝛ-ċeaꝫaꝛꝫa beaꝫa
oo cumaḋ aꝫuꝛ oo ceaꝛaḋ ꝛe h-aꝫaıḋ tıonꝛꝫontóıꝛꝛıꝫeaḋ,
5 aꝫuꝛ ꝫo moꝛṁóꝛ ꝛe h-aꝫaıḋ leanaḃ aıꝛ a ꝫ-cláıꝛín, no
ꝛá'n tuaıꝛım ꝛın. Aċt, aıꝛ na ꝼoꝛꝫlaḋ, oo ċíꝛo ꝫo
ḃ-ꝼuılıo ḋa h-teanꝫaıḋ ann : aꝫuꝛ naċ ḃ-ꝼuıl aca, oá
ḃꝛıꝫ-ꝛın, aċt leaċ na h-oıḃꝛe ꝛe oeunaḋ : ꝛıonnꝛuıo ꝛe
oul ċꝛío, ꝫuꝛ aḃ ıomḋa ní ıꝛ an leaċ-ꝛo ꝼéın, naċ aꝛ
10 h-ollṁuıꝫeaḋ ċum muıꝛıꝫıne oo ċuꝛ aıꝛ an meaḃaıꝛ, aċ
oo ċum na tuıꝫꝛe oo ꝛoıllꝛıuꝫaḋ, aꝫuꝛ ċum na tola oo
ꝫluaꝛaċt ċum na ꝛuḃáılce oo ꝫnáıċ-ċleaċtaḋ, aꝫuꝛ an
ouḃáılce oo ꝼeaċnaḋ ; aꝫuꝛ ꝫo ḃ-ꝼuılıo ꝫníoṁa cumċa
caonoúċꝛaċta, aꝫuꝛ uꝛnaıꝫċe aċċumuıꝛe ꝛíoꝛ aꝫuꝛ ꝛuaꝛ
15 na ṁeaꝛꞡ, noċ ıꝛ ınoeunta a n-aımꝛꝛıḃ euꝫꝛaṁla, aꝫuꝛ
ꝫo h-áıꝛıꝫ ꝛoıṁe aꝫuꝛ a n-oıaıꝫ ꝼaoıꝛꝛoıne aꝫuꝛ cumaoıne,
aıꝛ maıoın aꝫuꝛ tꝛáċ-nóna, aꝫuꝛ ann amaıḃ eıle ; aıꝛ
ċoꝛ, ꝫo ḃ-ꝼóıꝛꝛıo ꝛé maꝛ leaḃꝛán-uꝛnaıꝫċe oo'n ṁuıntıꝛ
aꝫ ꝛaċ ḃ-ꝼuıl a ꝛáꝛuꝫaḋ, ná ꝛóꝛ móꝛán aımꝛꝛe aıꝛ a
20 láıṁ : Oo ċíꝛo maꝛ an ꝫ-céuona, ꝫo ḃ-ꝼuıl lán-ꝛúl ıꝛ an
ꝫ-clóḋ, aꝫuꝛ ꝫuꝛ caılleaḋ móꝛán ꝛáıꝛéıꝛ, tꝛe ꝛúıꝫıuꝫaḋ
ceaꝛoaḋ aꝫuꝛ ꝛꝛeaꝫaꝛtaḋ an oa ċeanꝫta ꝫo beaċt aꝛ
coınne a ċéıle ; aꝫuꝛ ꝫo ḃ-ꝼuıl cuıo ḋe aıꝛ na líonaḋ
ꝛé ꝛáıḋtıḃ o'n ꝫꝛꝛıḃınn Ohıaꝫa, etc., aꝫuꝛ ꝛe coṁꝼoclaıḃ
25 mínıꝫċe na ꝫaoıḋeılꝫe. ꝼá ḋeoıꝫ, teıꝫṁeoꝫuıo, aıꝛ oeıꝛeaḋ,
ꝛe h-aıċꝫıoꝛꝛa an teaꝫaıꝛꞡ Chꝛíoꝛouıże a n-oáꝛ aıꝛ na
ċumaḋ, tuılleaḋ ꝛe ceuo blıaḋaın o ꝛoın, le ḃonauentuꝛa
o h-Coouꝛa bꝛátaıꝛ oíoꝫꝛaıꝛeaċ, ꝛoꝫlumċa o'oꝛo San

ADVERTISEMENT.

I. THE Bulk of this *Catechism* will probably, at first View, afright such as are used only to little *Abridgments, meerly* calculated for *Beginners*, and *chiefly for Children at their Horn-book*, or thereabout. But, in opening it, they will find, it is in *two Languages*, and that, consequently, they have but *Half the Work* on their Hands: They will find by perusing it, that, in this *very Half*, there are several Things, not intended for charging the *Memory*, but for enlightening the *Understanding*, and moving the *Will* to the Practice of Virtue, and Flight of Vice; and that it is interspersed with short *Forms* of Acts of Devotion, and Prayers, to be used on different Occasions, and particularly before and after Confession and Communion, Morning and Evening, and at other Times; so, that it may serve as a Sort of *Prayer-book*, to such as have no better, nor much Time to spare: They will likewise see, that the Print is large, and much Waste occasioned, through the Necessity of placing the Questions and Answers of both Languages, directly opposite to each other; and that some Paper is taken up by Quotations from Scripture, &c. and by Synonymous or Explanatory *Irish* Words: Lastly they will, towards the End, meet with an Abridgment of the *Christian Doctrine* in *Irish* Rhyme, composed upwards of an Age ago by the zealous and learned F. *Bonaventure O Heoghusa* of the Order of S. *Francis;* and also with the Elements of the *Irish* Language, in Favour of such as would fain learn to read it; and

B 2

Phroinnsias: agus fós ré tosuiġiḃ na teangṫa Gaoiḋeilge, mar ġeall air an luċt ré ar mian a léiġeaḋ, ċum conganta re na g-coṁarsain: Áit fós, ann a d-tugṫar contus air son an leiṫid big do glacaḋ sios agus suas air feaḋ an leaḃair-se, do ṫaoḃ an nóis air a sgrioḃṫar Corp-focla agus Coirp-litreaċa Gaoiḋeilge. Giḋeaḋ, tar ċeann iomudaṁlaċta na neiṫeaḋ eugcosaṁla-sa, ní ḃ-fuil aoin-leaṫ don leaḃar-so, láiṁ re ḃeiṫ leaṫ coṁfada ris an teagasg do rinneaḋ suas an aoin-teangaiḋ aṁáin re h-orduġaḋ Choṁairle h-Trent, agus do diriġeaḋ ċum gaċ uile ḋuine air a ḃ-fuil coiṁeud anmann ċáiċ oile, da ġreamuġaḋ ḋioḃ a ṁúnaḋ do'n ṗobul iar na ċur is an teangaiḋ ċoitċinn: Ni, do ċiteadar, naċ ar ḃféidir do ḋeunaḋ go fóill a n-Éirinn.

Concil. Trid. Ses. 24. c. 7.

II. Agus go dearḃṫa is baoġlaċ agus is millteaċ an mearḃall tuataṁail tré measdar gur leór na ceud ṫosuiġe, do cuireaḋ a n-oireaṁuin d'aois ḃoig, ṁaoiṫ na leanaḃ, mar ṫeagasg do ḋaoiniḃ is ársuiġe ioná iad; no naċ beag an Chré, na h-Aiṫeanta, Urnaiġ an Tiġearna, agus anmanna aṁáin na seaċt sácramuinteaḋ agus na seaċt b-peacaiḋeaḋ marḃṫa a ráḋ do ṁeaḃair, air nós leanaḃ, gan fios a g-céille, ná a réime, ná fós na g-coinġioll a tá riaċtanaċ ċum na sácramuinteaḋ úd féin, noċ ṫaiṫiġid, do ġlacaḋ mar is cóir, giḋ gur air a n-glacaḋ go maiṫ tá a slánuġaḋ.

III. Ní foláir go deiṁin do na leiniḃ, naċ eugcruaiġe a g-colann ioná a g-ciall, agus fós do gaċ uile nuaiḋ-ṫionsgantóir na miontosuiġe-se d'fáġail a meaḃair, aṁuil do ġeiḃid an aibġidil, giḋ naċ d-tuigid iad; óir is buille air aġaiḋ é. Aċt is mór an daille agus an t-aḋḃar truaiġe agus gola a ṁear, gur dlisdionaċ dóiḃ fuireaċ na bun sin, no go ḃ-fuil fios a g-creidiṁ aca, agus gur féidir dóiḃ na sácramuinte do ġlacaḋ gan eolus is foirleaṫaduiġe ioná sin air na neiṫiḃ, do ḃeanas re sláinte an anma, eaḋon, air a n-dualgas do ṫaoḃ Dé,

thereby be useful to their Neighbour: Where likewise some little Latitude, taken here and there, throughout this Volume, touching the Manner of writing some *Irish* Words and Letters, is accounted for. Yet, notwithstanding this Variety of Subjects, no *one Half* of this Book is near *half* as long as the Catechism compiled, but in *one Language only*, by Order of the Council of *Trent*, and directed to all those, who have the Cure of Souls, with an Injunction to get it put into the *vulgar Tongue*, and *to teach it the People;* which, it seems, could not hitherto be done in *Ireland.*

Concil. Trid. Ses. 24. c. 7.

II. And certainly, it is a dangerous and pernicious *vulgar* Mistake to think, that the first Principles *only* of Religion, which are adapted to the *tender Age of Children*, are sufficient Instruction for Persons of riper Years; or that it is enough to say by Heart, *Children-like*, the *Creed*, *Commandments*, the *Lords Prayer*, and the Names *only* of *seven Sacraments*, and *seven deadly Sins*, without knowing either the Meaning or Extent thereof, or the necessary Dispositions for receiving *those very Sacraments*, which they frequent, and on the *Well-receiving* whereof, their Salvation doth depend.

III. *Children* indeed, whose Minds are as weak as their Bodies, and even all *Beginners* are to get, as they do the *Alphabet*, those little short *Catechisms* by Heart, although they do not understand them; for it is so much done. But to pretend, that they may *lawfully* stop there; or that they know *their Religion*, and can receive the *Sacraments* without a more extensive Knowledge of the Truths of Salvation, that is, of their Duty towards God, towards their Neighbour, and towards themselves, is a woful and deplorable Blindness. It is

do ṫaoḃ a g-coṁarsan, agus d'a d-taoḃ féin. Ní lúġa is diṫċéillíġe é ioná do ṁeas, gur féidir ré leiniḃ do beaṫuiġear re bainne, agus do ní láṁacán beag, biaḋ bríoġṁar do ḋíleáġaḋ, agus rioċ sios agus suas; nó go d-tig leo-san agus re tionsgantóiriḃ oile leaḃra do léiġeaḋ agus do ṫuigsin, an tan is eol dóiḃ an aibġitil aṁáin. Ní ṫig re macaoiṁiḃ foġlumṫa féin, eaḋon, re luct léiġinn, an Chré, na h-Aiṫeanta, ná na Sácramuinte do ṫuigsin, muna míniġṫear ḋóiḃ iad: Ní mó ioná sin is féidir ḋóiḃ socar air biṫ do ḃuain as na sácramuintiḃ, muna raḃaid ullṁuiġṫe, mar is dual, ċum a n-glacṫa: Ní féidir ḋóiḃ a ḃeiṫ ullmuiġṫe, mar is cóir, muna feas dóiḃ creud é an t-ullṁuġaḋ is riaċtanaċ: Ní féidir ḋóiḃ fios a ḃeiṫ aca air an ullṁuġaḋ-so muna múintear iad, mar a dliġṫear. Oir, is "tré "éisdeaċt do ṫig an creideaṁ" giḋ subáilce neaṁḋa é "agus tre ḃréiṫir Chriosd ṫigeas éisdeaċt;" is é sin ré ráḋ, gur o ḃeul na n-daoineaḋ do ġeiḃṫear fios na neiṫeaḋ is inċreidṫe agus is indeunta, maille re congnaṁ ġrásaḋ Dé.

Rom. 10. 17.

Uime so, do ċaiṫ ar Slánuiġṫeóir féin, an t-Ard-sagart Siorruiḋe, Aoḋaire agus Easbog ar n-anmann, mórán aimsire agus saoṫair ag múnaḋ na n-Absdol, agus na ḋiaiḋ sin, ag a g-cur "fá'n doṁan," do ġreamuiġ ḋíoḃ "na h-uile Chineaḋaċa do ṫeagasg, da "m-baisdeaḋ a n-ainim an Aṫar, agus an Mhic, agus an "Spioraid Naoiṁ;" agus do "ṁunaḋ ḋóiḃ gaċ uile ni "dar aiṫin se ḋíoḃ-san do ċoiṁeud."

S. Mat. 28. 19, 20.

Is riaċtanaċ mar so, an drong, do ṫig ċum céille, do ṁúnaḋ; ni foláir ḋóiḃ briaṫar Dé do ċlos, agus na neiṫe úd d'ḟoġluim, noċ a ta d'ḟiaċaiḃ orṫa do ċreideaṁuin agus do ċoiṁeud; agus fós ni foláir ḋóiḃ foġlum cionnas is cóir a g-coiṁeud; gan sin, aṁuil mar ċruṫuiġeas gníoṁ go laeṫeaṁul, ni féidir ḋóiḃ, da maḋ Eigse iad, fios na rúindiaṁar, ta is an g-Cré, ná na sliġṫeaḋ iomadaṁla re m-brisdear na h-aiṫeanta, a ḃeiṫ aca: is lúġa ioná

as unreasonable as to think, that Children, who live upon *milk only*, and *learn to stand*, or walk a *little*, can also digest *solid Food*, and *run about;* or that they and other Beginners can read and understand Books, when they know *only* the *Alphabet*. Scholars *themselves*, that is, Men of Literature, are not able to understand either the *Creed*, or *Commandments*, or *Sacraments*, unless they be expounded for them; neither can they reap any Benefit by the *Sacraments*, except they be *well disposed* to approach them : Nor can they be well disposed without knowing the *necessary Dispositions* : Nor can they *Rom. 10.* know these Dispositions unless they be *duly instructed.* *17.* For, *Faith*, although a *Supernatural* Virtue, *comes by Hearing, and Hearing by the Word of Christ;* that is to say, the Knowledge of the Things to be beleived and practised, with the Assistance of the Divine Grace, comes by the Ministry of Men; wherefore our *Saviour, the Eternal High Priest, the Pastor and Bishop of our Souls,* employed much Time and Labour to instruct his *Apostles ;* and afterwards commanded them, in giving them their *Mission*, to *instruct all Nations, baptizing them in the Name of the Father, and of the Son, and of the Holy Ghost ;* and to *S. Mat.* *teach them to OBSERVE ALL THINGS WHATSOEVER he had* *28. 19, 20.* *commanded them.* People then, come to the Use of Reason, ought necessarily to be instructed; they must hear the Word of God, and learn what they are to believe and observe, and *even* learn how to observe it; otherwise, as daily Experience proves it, they cannot, were they *Philosophers*, know, as they ought, the *Mysteries* contained in the *Creed ;* nor the various Ways of transgressing the *Commandments ;* much less the Meaning, Force and Effect of the *Sacraments ;* nor the Dispositions necessary for receiving them. Neither can they know the great Obligations, they contract in receiving them : Nor the Necessity,

1 sin is féidir dóibh fios a bheith aca, creud is ciall, bríg,
agus toradh do na sácramuintibh; no creud e an
t-ullmhughadh is piactanach chum a ngltacha: Ní mó ioná
sin is féidir dóibh fios a bheith aca, creud e an t-ualach, do
5 ghabhaid orra féin, an tan do ghlacaid na sácramuinte; ná
creud é piactanus, coingioll agus tairbe na n-urnaighte,
muna múintear dóibh iad go maith, air flighe éigin.

IV.   A noir, mádh is e ro cor na n-daoineadh tuigsionacha,
foghlumtha féin, is dearbhtha nach féidir do'n mhuintir, a ta
10 gan léigionn, gan eólus, fios na neiteadh piactanacha-so,
ná, dá bríg sin, fios a g-creidimh beith aca, gidh go
n-deuraidir, do mheadhair go beacht, an Chré, na
h-Aiteanta, na Sácramuinte, &c. muna minigtear dóibh
iad go rotuigsionach agus go lionmhar, agus fós muna
15 g-cuirtear do dheoin no air éigean a g-céill dóibh iad:
is fios nach uras ro dheunadh, agus nach foláir mórán
saothair agus foighde do ghlacadh; gidheadh a ta ré
piactanach: is mó ioná sin uile, is fiú an t-anam: do
choruin ré níos mó go mór do Mhac Dé: "Do

1 Cor.
6. 20.

20 "ceannuigheadh sinn uile," deir an t-Abhstal, "air luach
"mór": gidheadh ní foghanfuidh an fuarghladh mór-so, eadhon,
bás agus ceusadh Iosa Criost, do'n dream a ta aineólach
is an g-creideamh, agus do chomhnuigheas ann a n-ainebhfios:
Caithfid a saoghal, agus do gheabhuid bás a b-peacadh, gidh
25 ghlacaid na sácramuinte: is mó an tarcuisne agus an
mhioclu do bheurain, agus an docharr do dheunain d' Eaglais
Dé, re na m-beatha agus re na m-beuraibh truaillighte,
ioná gach ancáineadh gráineamhuil da rgeitid amach na
h-lúduighe, na Turcaigh, agus víttreidmheacha oile go
30 laeteamhuil na h-agaid; óir ní b-fuil ní air bit is mó
marluigheas Criost agus a Naomh-ceile, an Eagluir, ioná
droichiomchar oilbéimeach anmóráin do na Catoilicibh; dá
b-fuil cuid, mar is ro feargach, faraor, do chách, tugta
do chraos, no d'oladán: cuid, do mhallúigheas agus do
35 mhionnuigheas go diorruighte, víttéillig: cuid aca, graosda

Conditions, and great Benefit of *Prayer*, except they be well instructed therein, one Way or other.

IV.   Now, if this be the Case *even of Men of Wit and Learning*, surely the unlearned and *ignorant People* cannot know *these necessary Truths*, nor consequently *their Religion*, although they should *punctually* say, by Heart, the *Creed*, *Commandments*, *Sacraments*, *&c.* unless they be familiarly and frequently explained, and *even forced, as it were, into their Heads*. It is true, that this is no easy Task ; and that it requires much Labour and Patience ; but that is necessary ; a Soul is worth more than all that ; it cost the *Son of God* a great Deal more ; we are all *bought*, saith the *Apostle, with a great Price.* Yet this great Ransom, the *Death and Passion* of *JESUS CHRIST*, will be of no Use to such as know not their Religion, and remain in Ignorance : They will, although they approach the *Sacraments*, live and die in Sin : They will by their corrupt Life and Manners, dishonour and asperse the *Church of God ;* and do *her* more Harm, than the horrid Blasphemies, which *Jews, Turks,* and other *Unbelievers* vomit out daily against her ; there being Nothing more injurious to *Christ* and his *holy Spouse,* than the wicked and scandalous Behaviour of too many *Catholicks;* whereof some, as it is too well known, are Drunkards or Tiplers : Some do curse and swear at Random : Some are openly lewd and shamelessly lascivious : Some Slanderers, great Lyars, and Sharpers : Many are proud, cholerick, quarrelsom and revengeful to a *high Degree :* Some overreach their Neighbour, and take away his *Goods,* as often as they imagine, they can do it without worldly Inconvenience : And many, are openly tied to, and

1 Cor. 6. 20.

1 óɼ áıp'o, aʒuɼ opúıɼeaṁuıl ʒo mıonáıpeaċ: cuıo ıċıom-
páıóċeaċ, ɼo ḃɼeuʒaċ, cealʒaċ: cuıo óıoḃ uaıḃɼeaċ, ſeaɼ-
ʒaċ, ḃɼúıʒneaċ, aınoıoʒalcaċ: cuıo oıle, oo ṁeallaɼ aʒuɼ
ſlaoaɼ a ʒ-coṁaɼɼa coıṁmınıc aʒuɼ ṁeaɼuıo, ʒo ɼaċaıo
5 ɼé leo ʒan mıoċoṁʒaɼ aıɼ a ċ-ɼaoʒal-ɼo: Aʒuɼ a ċá an
ıomaɼcaıo óıoḃ ceanʒaılce ʒo ſollaɼ oo neıċıḃ ɼaoʒalca,
aʒuɼ aʒ ɼıoċ na n-oıaıo coṁamplaċ ɼe Cuɼcuıʒ aʒuɼ
ɼáʒánuıʒ.

V.   Ʒıõeaó oo níõ na Caċoılıcıʒe loċċaċa-ɼo uıle, aıɼ nóɼ
Rom. 2. 10 na n-luoaıʒeaó "maoıõɼeaċuɼ aɼ an olıʒeaó, aʒuɼ cɼé
23.   "ḃɼıɼeaó an olıʒıo caɼcuıɼnıʒıo Oıa," aʒuɼ an Eaʒluıɼ.
Maoıõıo, ʒuɼ clann oo'n eaʒluıɼ ſıɼe ıao; aʒuɼ ʒo
o-cuʒaıo, uaıɼ ɼa m-blıaóaın, uɼɼaım éıʒın, aʒuɼ ceıɼ-
beánaó aıċɼıʒe uaóċa; aċ "ní ċuʒaıo aon-coɼaó, ıɼ
S. Luc. 15 "ıomċuḃaıo õoɼ aıċɼıʒe, uaóċa:" A ḃ-ſao uaó, oo ċéıo,
3. 8.   maɼ ɼo, o ḃlıaóaın ʒo ḃlıaóuın, aʒ cáɼnaó ɼeaċaıo aıɼ
ɼeaċaó, ualaıʒ aıɼ ualaċ, aʒ cuıcım aʒuɼ aʒ éıɼʒe,
máõ ıɼ ſıoɼ õóıḃ, ʒan leaɼuʒaó ɼoılléıɼ aıɼ bıċ no ʒo
o-cıʒıõ an báɼ ʒan ſıoɼ oɼċa: Ní oo ḃeıɼ cıonſáċa
20 oo õɼunʒaıḃ áıɼıʒe a ɼáõ, ʒo o-cuʒann an Eaʒluıɼ
1 Tim. Caċoılıce Uɼɼa aʒuɼ Oaınʒean na Fıɼınne, ceaõ ɼeaċaıo
3. 15.   õúınn; ʒıõ ıɼ ſollaɼ ʒuɼ aḃ é aınḃɼıoɼ aʒuɼ oaılle coõċa
oa cloınn õɼoḃláɼaıʒ ıɼ cıonċaċ ɼıɼ an neaṁċɼáḃaó
uaċḃaɼaċ-ɼo oo ċuɼ na leıċ: aʒuɼ náċ é a ceaʒaɼʒ-ɼan
25 ıɼ aõḃaɼ õó; oıɼ a ca ɼé coṁʒlan coıṁneaṁʒɼonaċ aʒuɼ
oo ſuaıɼ ɼı é o na Cuıɼmıʒċeoıɼ aʒuɼ a Cúṁouıʒċeoıɼ
Neaṁoa Ioɼa Cɼíoɼo; aṁuıl ḃuɼ ſollaɼ oo'n oɼoınʒ oo
ʒlacſaɼ a láıṁ, ʒan ſuaċ nó ʒɼáõ, a ʒéaɼ-loɼʒ, ſóɼ ıɼ
an mıon-cɼaoċaɼ-ɼo aɼ n-oıaıo. '

VI. 30 Aʒuɼ, ċum ʒan a ʒ-cuɼ níoɼ ſaıoe aıɼ cáıɼoe, oa
ċaoḃ ɼo: ceaʒaɼʒaıo ɼı ʒan ɼʒuɼ, ʒan ċlaoċló, "ʒan
S. Math. "ní naoṁċa oo ċaḃaıɼc oo ṁaoɼuıʒıḃ; aʒuɼ ʒan cloċa
7. 6.   "uaıɼle oo ċeılʒıon a ḃɼıaónuıɼe na muc," eaõon, ʒan na
ɼáċɼamuınce oo ċaḃaıɼc oo'n oɼeam naċ aɼ múıneaõ,
35 maɼ ıɼ oual; naċ ḃ-ſuıl ſıoɼ-õoılʒıoɼaċ aʒuɼ ulláṁuıʒċe

run after the Things of this Life, as eagerly as *Mahometans* and *Heathens*.

V.   Still, all *these vicious Catholicks* do, *Jew-like, boast of the Law, and by prevaricating the Law, dishonour God* and his *Church*. They boast of being *Children* of the *true Church*, and of making, once a Year, some Submission and *Shew* of Repentance; yet *bring forth* little or *no worthy Fruits of Penance:* On the contrary, they generally go on so, from Year to Year, adding Sin to Sin, Load to Load, falling and rising, as they pretend, without any visible Amendment of Life, until Death surprizes them; which gives some People Occasion to say, that the *Catholick Church, the Pillar and Ground of Truth,* gives us *Leave to commit Sin;* although it is manifest, that it is the Ignorance and Blindness *only* of some of her Licentious Children, that furnish a Handle to upbraid her with this *monstrous Impiety;* and not, at all, *her Doctrine,* which is always as *pure and spotless* as *her Divine Founder, JESUS CHRIST,* delivered it to her; as it shall clearly appear to such as will, without Prevention, take Pains to examine it, *even* in this little Work. *Rom. 22. 23.* *S. Luc. 3. 8.* *1 Tim. 3. 15.*

VI.   And not to send them farther off, touching this Point: Her *constant* and *invariable Doctrine* is, *never to give that, which is holy, to Dogs; nor to cast Pearls before Swine;* that is, not to administer the *Sacraments* to such as are not *duly instructed, penitent,* and *well prepared;* not *even Baptism it self,* to such as have the *S. Mat. 7. 6.*

1 ᵹo mᴀiċ; ᵹᴀn ᴦóᴦ ᴀn bᴀiᴦᴅeᴀú ᵱéin, ᴅo ċᴀbᴀiᴘᴄ ᴅo'n
ṁuinᴄiᴘ, ᴅo ċᴀiniᵹ ċum céille: ᴀᵹuᴦ ᴅ'ᴀ ᴅ-ᴄᴀoḃᴘoin ᴀ
ᴅeiᴘ ᴦí, "nᴀċ ᴦoláiᴘ ᴅóiḃ ḃeiċ ᴀiᴘ nᴀ ᴅ-ᴄeᴀᵹᴀᴦᵹ, ᴀᵹuᴦ
"nᴀ neiċe, ᴅ'ᴦóillᴘᵹ ᴀᵹuᴦ ᴅo ᵹeᴀll Ɔiᴀ, ᴅo ċᴘeiᴅeᴀú
5 "mᴀille ᴘe conᵹnᴀṁ nᴀ n-ᵹᴘáᴦ neᴀṁᴅᴀ; ᴀᵹuᴦ ᴄᴀᴘ ᵹᴀċ
Conc. "ní, ᵹuᴘ ᴀb é Ɔiᴀ, ᴅo ᴦᴀoᴘᴀᴦ ᴘe nᴀ ᵹᴘᴀᴦᴀiḃ ᴀn ᴘeᴀcᴀċ,
Trid. Ses. "ᴄᴘeᴦ ᴀn ḃ-ᴦuᴀᴦᵹlᴀú ᴅo ᴘinneᴀú ᴘe h-íoᴦᴀ Cᴘíoᴦᴅ: ᵹuᴘ
6. c. 6. "cóiᴘ ᴅóiḃ, ᴀiᴘ ᴄuiᵹᴘin ᴅóiḃ, ᵹo ḃ-ᴦuiliᴅ ᴀ b-ᴘeᴀcᴀú,
Ses. 24. "cᴘioᴄnuᵹᴀú ᴘoiṁ ċeiᴘᴄ-ḃᴘeiᴄeᴀṁnuᴘ Ɔé; Súil ᴅo
c. 7. 10 "ċᴀbᴀiᴘᴄ ᴦuᴀᴦ ᴀiᴘ ċᴘócᴀiᴘe ᴀn Ꞇiᵹeᴀᴘnᴀ, ᴅóċċᴀᴦ ᴀᵹuᴦ
"muiniᵹin ᴅo ḃeiċ ᴀcᴀ, ᵹo m-biᴀú ᴄᴘócᴀiᴘeᴀċ leo, ᴀiᴘ
"ᴦon Cᴘíoᴦᴅ; ᴀᵹuᴦ ᴄionᴦᵹnᴀú ᴀiᴘ Ɔhiᴀ ᴅo ᵹᴘáᴅuᵹᴀú,
"mᴀᴘ h-ᴄoḃᴀᴘ nᴀ h-uile ᴦiᴘeunᴄᴀċᴄᴀ. Oᴦ ᴀ ċionn ᴦin,
"ní ᴦoláiᴘ ᴅóiḃ ᴦuᴀċ ᴀᵹuᴦ ᵹᴘáin ᴅo ḃeiċ ᴀcᴀ ᴀiᴘ ᴀn
15 "b-ᴘeᴀcᴀú, eᴀúon, ᴀn ᴀiċᴘiᵹe úᴅ, iᴦ ᴘiᴀċᴄᴀnᴀċ ᴘoiṁ
"bᴀiᴦᴅeᴀú, ᴅo úeunᴀú. ᵱᴀ úeoiᴅ, ᵹo ḃ-ᴦuil ᴅ'uᴀlᴀċ
"oᴘċᴀ, ᴀn ᴄᴀn ᴅo ċuiᴘiᴅ ᴘompᴀ bᴀiᴦᴅeᴀú ᴅo ᵹlᴀcᴀú,
"nuᴀiᴅ-beᴀċᴀ ᴅo ċoᴦuᵹᴀú, ᴀᵹuᴦ nᴀ h-ᴀiᴄeᴀnᴄᴀ ᴅo
"ċoiṁlíonᴀú. Iᴦ ᴄᴀᴘ éiᴦ ᴀn ullṁuiᵹᴄe-ᴦe," ᴀᵹuᴦ ᵹo
20 coiċcionn, ᴄᴀᴘ éiᴦ "ᴅiulᴄᴀú óᴦ ᴀiᴅᴅ ᴅ'ollᴀᴦ ᴀᵹuᴦ ᴅ'oiḃᴘiḃ
"ᴀn ᴅiᴀbuil, ᴅo ᴄíᵹ ᴀn ᴦiᴘeunᴄᴀċᴄ ᵱéin, noċ ᴅo ċiᴀl-
"luiᵹeᴀᴦ ni h-e ᴀṁáin mᴀiċeᴀṁnuᴘ nᴀ b-ᴘeᴀcᴀú, ᴀċᴄ
"ᴦóᴦ nᴀoṁᴀú, ᴀᵹuᴦ ᴀᴄnuᴀúuᵹᴀú ᴀn ᴅuine ᴄᴀoḃ ᴀ ᴦuiᵹ,
"ᴄᴘé ᵹlᴀcᴀú ᵹᴘáᴦ ᴀᵹuᴦ h-ᴄíoúlᴀiceᴀú ᴀn Sᴘioᴦᴀiᴅ Ոᴀoiṁ
25 "ᵹo ᴄoilᴄeᴀnᴀċ." Ᵹo nuiᵹe ᴦo ᴦoiᴘᴄiᴅiol nᴀ h-eᴀᵹluiᴦe,
ᴅo ċᴀoḃ bᴀiᴘᴅiú nᴀ ᴅᴘoinᵹe ᴅo ċᴀiniᵹ ċum ᴄuiᵹᴦe.

VII. Ɔo ċᴀoḃ nᴀ muinᴄiᴘe, "ᴅo ċuiᴄ, ᴦóᴦ ᴄᴀᴘ éiᴦ ᵹuᴘ
"ᴦoillᴘᵹeᴀú iᴀᴅ ᴀon uᴀiᴘ ᴀṁáin, ᴀᵹuᴦ ᵹuᴘ ḃlᴀiᴘᴅuᴅᴀᴘ
Heb. 6. "ᴀn ᴄíoúlᴀice neᴀṁᴅᴀ, ᴀᵹuᴦ ᵹuᴘ ᴘoinneᴀú ᴀn Sᴘioᴘᴀᴅ
4, 5, 6. 30 "Ոᴀoṁ leo," múiniᴅ ᴀn Eᴀᵹluiᴘ Cᴀᴄoilice, nᴀċ ᴦoláiᴘ
ᴅóiḃ níoᴦ mó ᵹo móᴘ ioná ᴀn ᴄ-ullṁuᵹᴀú ᴘeuṁᴘáiᴅᴄe iᴦ
Conc. ᴘiᴀċᴄᴀnᴀċ ᴘoiṁ bᴀiᴦᴅeᴀú; "nᴀc ᴦoláiᴘ ᴀ n-ᴀiċᴘiᵹe ᴀ ḃeiċ
Trid. Ses. "euᵹcoᴘṁuil ᴘe h-ᴀiċᴘiᵹe ᴀn ḃᴀiᴘᴅiú; nᴀċ ᵱéiᴅiᴘ ᴀiᴘ ᴀon-
6. c. 14. "ċoᴘ ᴀ n-ᴀᴄᵱuiᴅiuᵹeᴀú ᴀᵹuᴦ ᴀ n-ᴀᴄnuᴀúuᵹᴀú ᴀ m-beᴀċᴀ
Ses. 14. "nᴀ n-ᵹᴘáᴦ ᵹᴀn ᴅoḃᴘón cᴘoiúe, ᴀᵹuᴦ ᵹᴘáin ᴀiᴘ ᴀ b-ᴘeᴀ-
c. 2, 3, 4. 35

Use of Reason ; and touching whom she teacheth, that *Conc.* *Trid. Ses.* *they are to be instructed and to believe, by the Assistance of* *6. c. 6.* *the Divine Grace, the Things, which God revealed and* *Ses. 24. c.* *promised ; and chiefly, that it is God, who by his Grace,* *7, de Re-* *form.* *Justifieth the Sinner, by the Redemption, which is in CHRIST* *JESUS : That understanding themselves to be Sinners, they* *are to fear the Divine Justice ; to look towards the Mercy of* *God ; to hope and confide, that he will be merciful to them* *for Christ's Sake ; and to begin to love God, as the Fountain* *of all Justice.*

Moreover *they are to conceive a Hatred and Detestation* *of Sin, viz. To do that Penance, which is requisite to be done* *Conc.* *before Baptism.* Lastly that, *during the Time they design to* *Trid. Ses.* *6. ib.* *receive Baptism, they are to begin a new Life, and to keep the* *Commandments.* After this Preparation, and ordinarily, *Ritual.* after a *publick Renunciation of all the Pomps and Works of* *Rom.* *Satan, ensueth Righteousness it self, which is not only a* *Remission of Sins, but also the Sanctification and Renewing* *Conc.* *of the inward Man, by a voluntary Receiving of the Grace and* *Trid. ib.* *Gifts of the Holy Ghost.* Thus far the *Church,* concerning the *Baptism* of *Adults.*

VII.   As to those, who, after *they have been once enlightened,* *Heb. 6.* *have also tasted the Heavenly Gift, and have been made* *4, 5, 6.* *Partakers of the Holy Ghost, and, yet, are fallen ;* the *Catholick Church* teacheth that a great Deal more than the above mentioned necessary Preparation for *Baptism,* is required of them; that their Penance ought to be *very* *Conc.* *different from that of Baptism ;* that *they cannot at all be* *Trid. Ses.* *6. c. 14.* *re-established and renewed to the Life of Grace, without a* *Ses. 14.* *hearty Sorrow and Hatred of past Offences ; not even without* *cc. 2, 3, 4.*

22   ᵱoᵱᵱhóṡᵱᴀ.

1 " cᴀιὐιḃ; ná ᵱóᵱ ṡᴀn móᵱán ᴠoċᴀιᵱ ᴀṡuᵱ ᴠoιlṡíᵱ; ná ṡᴀn
" ᵱún neᴀᵱcṁᴀᵱ ᴀn ᵱeᴀcᴀὐ ᴠo ᵱeᴀċnᴀὐ o ᵱιn ᵱuᴀᵱ, ᴀιᵱ
" m-beιċ ᴠ'ᵱίᵱ-ċeᴀᵱc 'Ỻé ᴠᴀ ṡᵱeᴀmuṡᴀὐ ᵱo ὐιoḃ. Ủιme

Conc. Trid. ib. c. 5.   " ᵱιn, nᴀċ ṡᴀn ᴀὐḃᴀᵱ ᴠo ṡoιᵱιᴠ nᴀ h-ᴀιċᵱeᴀċᴀ nᴀoṁċᴀ
5 " bᴀιᵱᴠeᴀὐ ᴀnᴀcιᴀċ ᴠo'n ᴀιċᵱιṡe." Ϻι h-e ᵱo ᵱóᵱ ᴀn
cᴀ-ιomlán ᴠᴀ n-ιᴀᵱᵱċᴀᵱ ᴀιᵱ " ᴀn ᴠᵱoιnṡ ᴀ cᴀ, cᴀᵱ éιᵱ
" ṡuᵱ ṡᴀḃᴀᴠᴀᵱ Cᵱίoᵱᴠ ιompᴀ, ᴀṡuᵱ ṡo n-ᴠeáᵱnᴀὐ Ϻuᴀὐ-
" ὐúιl ιonn-ᵱᴀn ᴠιoḃ," coιṁᴠιomḃuιὐeᴀċ ᵱιn ᴀṡuᵱ cᵱoιᴠ
ᴀ n-ᴀṡᴀιὐ 'Ỻé ṁóιᵱ nᴀ n-uιle Chuṁᴀċcᴀὐ: " Ϻι ᵱéιᴠιᵱ
10 " ὐóιḃ (ᴀᵱ ᴀn Eᴀṡluιᵱ) mᴀιċeᴀṁnuᵱ ᴠ'ᵱáṡᴀιl ᴀnn ᴀoιn-
" ᵱeᴀcᴀὐ mᴀᵱḃċᴀ, munᴀ ḃ-ᵱoιllᵱιṡιᴠ, ᴀn cᴀn ιᵱ ᵱéιᴠιᵱ
" leo, ṡᴀċ uιle ᵱeᴀcᴀὐ mᴀᵱḃċᴀ ιᵱ ᵱeᴀᵱᴀċ ὐóιḃ, cᴀᵱ éιᵱ
" ᴀ ṡ-coṡuᴀιᵱ ᴠo ṁιonċuᴀᵱcuṡᴀὐ; ᵱóᵱ nᴀ ᵱeᴀcᴀιὐe ᴠo
" ᵱιnneᴀᴠᴀᵱ ᵱe ᵱmuᴀιneᴀὐ ᴀṡuᵱ mιᴀnṡuᵱ ᴀṁáιn, noċ ιᵱ
15 " ᴠoιṁne, ᴀιᵱ uᴀιᵱιḃ, ᴠo loιceᴀᵱ ᴀn c-ᴀnᴀm, ᴀṡuᵱ ιᵱ
" bᴀoṡluιṡe ιoná nᴀ ᵱeᴀcᴀιὐe ᴠo nιċeᴀᵱ óᵱ áιᴠo;" munᴀ
ḃ-ᵱoιllᵱιṡιᴠ ιᴀᴠ (ᴀᵱ ᴀn Eᴀṡluιᵱ) " ṡo ᵱoιlléιᵱ, ᴀὐnᴀιᵱeᴀċ
" ᴠo'n ᴠᵱeᴀm le ᴀ n-ᴠúḃᴀιᵱc Cᵱίoᵱᴠ: ṡᴀḃᴀιὐ-ᵱι ᴀn

S. Jo. 20. 22, 23.   " Sᵱιoᵱᴀᴠ Ϻᴀoṁ: ṡιὐ bé ᴠᴀ mᴀιċᵱιὐ ᵱḃ ᴀ b-ᵱeᴀcᴀιὐe ᴀ
20 " cáιᴠ ᵱιᴀᴠ mᴀιċᵱeᴀċ ᴀcᴀ; ᴀṡuᵱ ṡιὐ bé ᴠᴀ ṡ-ceᴀnṡólċᴀoι
" ᴀ b-ᵱeᴀcᴀιὐe, ᴀ cáιᴠ ᵱιᴀᴠ ceᴀnṡᴀιlce." Ϻι ᴠlιṡċeᴀᵱ
ὐóιḃ, ᵱóᵱ cᴀᵱι éιᵱ ᴀn ᵱᴀoιᵱᴠιn oιᵱίᵱeᴀl, ιoċᵱláιn-
ceᴀċ-ᵱo ᴠo ὐeunᴀὐ, ᴀṡuᵱ cᴀᵱ éιᵱ ṡᴀċ coṁᴀᵱċᴀ ᵱιoᵱ-
ᴀιċᵱeᴀċuιᵱ, ιᵱ ιmιᴀᵱᵱcᴀ ṡo céιllιṡe oᵱċᴀ, ᴠo ċᴀιᵱbeánᴀὐ

Conc. Trid. ib. c. 3. & 8.   25 " ᴀn ᴀḃᵱolóιᴠ, ᴀnn ᴀ ḃ-ᵱuιl ṡo bunuὐᴀᵱᴀċ bᵱιιṡ h-ᵱᴀc-
" ᵱᴀmuιnce nᴀ h-ᴀιċᵱιṡe," ᴠ'ᵱáṡᴀιl, no ṡo n-ṡéιllιᴠ
ṡo h-oιᵱίᵱιol, " ᴀṡuᵱ ṡo n-ᴀoncuιṡιᴠ ᴠ'oιḃᵱeᴀċᴀιḃ ᴀn
" leoιᵱṡníoṁᴀ ᴀṡuᵱ nᴀ h-ᴀιċᵱιṡe, eᴀᴠon, cᵱoᵱṡᴀὐ, ὐéιᵱc,
" uᵱnᴀιṡ, etc. noċ ᴠo ṡᵱeᴀmuιṡċeᴀᵱ ὐιoḃ, nι h-e ᴀṁáιn
30 " ċum ᴀ n-ᴠᵱoιċċleᴀċcᴀὐ ᴠo ᵱṡᵱιoᵱ, ᴀṡuᵱ ᴀ ṡ-cuᵱ ᴀιᵱ ᴀ
" ṡ-coιṁeuᴠ ᴀṡuᵱ ᴀιᵱ ᴀ n-ᴀιᵱe níoᵱ ᵱeáᵱᵱ, o ᵱιn ᵱuᴀᵱ, ᴀ.
" n-ᴀṡᴀιὐ ᴀccuιcιme cubᴀιᵱcίṡ; ᴀċc ᵱóᵱ ċum nᴀ coιᵱce
" ċuᴀιὐ ċoᵱc, ᴠo ὐιoṡᴀιlc. Ꭺṡuᵱ ṡo ᴠeιṁιn, (ᴠeιᵱ ᵱóᵱ ᴀn
" Eᴀṡluιᵱ) ᴠo ċιceᴀᵱ nᴀċ oιᵱeᴀṁnᴀċ ᴠo ċeιᵱc-ḃᵱeιceᴀṁnuᵱ
35 " 'Ỻé, ᴀn ᴠᵱeᴀm, ᴠo ċιoncuιṡ, cᵱe ᴀιnḃᵱιoᵱ, ᵱoιṁ bᴀιᵱᴠeᴀὐ,

*great Pains and Lamentations ; nor without a firm Purpose
of sinning no more, the Divine Justice requiring, it should
be so.* Hence *Penance is, by the holy Fathers, deservedly
called a painful Baptism.* Neither is this all, that is required of such as are so *ungrateful, after they have put on
Christ, and were by Baptism, made a new Creature in him,* as
to offend the *Divine Majesty :* They cannot (continues the   *Conc.*
Church) *obtain the Remission of any mortal Sin, without*   *Trid. ib.*
declaring, when they can, all the mortal Sins, which after a   *c. 5.*
diligent Examination, they *are conscious* of; even *the Sins
of Thought and Desire, which do sometimes wound the Soul
deeper, and are more dangerous than those that are openly
committed ; without declaring all* (the *Church* sayeth) *plainly
and modestly before those,* to whom *Christ* said : *Receive ye*   *S. John.*
the holy Ghost : Whose Sins ye shall forgive, they are for-   *20. 22, 23.*
given them ; and whose Sins ye shall retain they are retained.
Nor are they *even* after this humbling and wholesom
Confession, and after giving all the Marks of sincere
Repentance, that Prudence can require, to receive *Absolu-*
tion, wherein the Force of the Sacrament of Penance, doth   *Conc. ib.*
chiefly consist, until they humbly submit to, and accept the   *c. 3. & 8.*
*Satisfactory, or Penetential Works, as Fasting, Alms-deeds,
Prayers, &c. which shall be enjoined them, in order not only
to destroy their vicious Habits, and make them more cautious
and vigilant, for the Future,* against *fatal Relapses ;* but also
in Punishment of *past Transgressions. And indeed* (the
Church speaks) *the Oeconomy or Order of the Divine Justice*   *Conc.*
seems to require, that those, who have, out of Ignorance, sinned *Trid. ib.*
                                                                  c. 8.

[*before*

1 " vo ġlacaḋ ḟaoi na rġéiṫ aip aon ṫ-rliġe ḟir an vpoing
" úv, vo ḃi coṁdána ḟin aġur ṫeampoll no ionaṽ coṁnuiġe
" Dé vo ṫruailliuġaḋ, aġur iarġnó vo ċur ġo ḃ-ḟior
" vóiḃ, aip an Spiopaṽ Naoṁ, ṫar éir ġur ḟuarġlaḋ iaṽ o
5 " ḋaor-ṁaċṫ an ḟeacaiṽ aġur an viaḃuil, aġur ġur
" ġlacavar ṫíoṽlaice an Spiopaiṽ Naoṁ."

VIII.

Conc.
Trid. ib.
c. 8.

S. Car.
Bor. Act.
Part. 4.
Instruct.
Confess.
Decr. In-
noc. Pap.
XI. 2.
Mart.
1679.

Aġ rin ṫeaġurġ na h-Eaġluiṫe Caṫoilice, aip na coiṁ-
ṫionól a v-Ṫpenṫ; ni vo ṫaoḃ na muinṫipe a ṫa oilḃéiṁeaċ
aġur vpoiċḃeuraċ ór áipv; óip ṫar cionn an iomláin ve
10 ro, opvuiġe-ri iaṽ-ro vo ċur ḟaoi ḃreiṫeaṁnur aiṫpiġe
oiṫeaċṫuir, vo ṗéir h-ṫoile an earḃoiġ: Ná róp vo ṫaoḃ
na ḃ-peacaċ ċpuaḋ-ṁuinéalaċa coṁnuiġear ann a miġ-
nioṁaiḃ aġur a ḃ-ḟailliġe coipṫeaċ a n-vualġaip, v'aiṁ-
ḋeóin ġur ġeallavar ġo meinic aipoc aġur aiṫpiġe vo
15 ḋeunaṽ; óip conġṁuiġe ri iaṽ-ro uile o coṁpoinn na
ráṫpamuinṫeaḋ, no ġo ġ-ċpuṫuiġiv ṗe na n-ġnioṁaṫaiḃ,
ġo n-veunaiv aiṫpiġe va ṗíṗiḃ; aġur ġo n-aṫpuiġiv a
m-beupa: Aċṫ róp vo ṫaoḃ na h-uile ṽpoinġe, vo ḟaoil-
ṫear vo ċáċ a ḃeiṫ cneaṫva, ġiṽeaṽ vo ṫruailliġ ġo
20 vaoiṫeaṁuil, ṫar éir ṫeaċṫ ċum ṫuiġṫe uilc aġur maiṫeara,
an ġloine aġur an rġéiṁ inṁeaṽónaċ úv, vo ḟuaravar
ṫpé ġpara an ḃaiṫroiv: aġur ionnar naċ ḟaċaṽ an ċuiv-re
va ḟoipċeaṽal aip aon-ċor ḟaoi láp; aġur naċ m-biaṽ
aoin-neaċ aineólaċ na ṫaoḃ, vo ḃriġ ġur aḃ aip eolur
25 ro, aġur aip a ċur a ġnioṁ, mar ir vual, a ṫa rlanuġaṽ
ḟurṁóip an voṁain; ġreamuiġe ri, aip ṫúp, vo na h-uile
oiviġiḃ ḟaoirvoine ḃreiṫeaṁnur aiṫpiġe vo ċur aip luċṫ
na h-aiṫpiġe vo ṗéir ġné a ḃ-peacaṽ, aġur a ġ-cumair
no a néipṫ ċum a coiṁlionṫa; aip eaġla, ġo m-beivir
30 rann-ṗáipṫeaċ a ḃ-peacaiṽiḃ ċáiċ oile, ṗa na ḃ-peacaiṽe
vo léiġion ṫopṫa ġo péiġ, aġur ṗa ḃeiṫ ro ḟéiṁ ḟir an
aiṫpiġeaċ. Ir an vara ḟeaċṫ, opvuiġe-ri a mílṫiḃ v'áiṫiḃ,
aġur ġo h-áipiġe ir an ṫeaġurġ Cpiorvuiġe ḟiop-ṁaiṫ,
ḟoipleiṫeaṽaċ úv, vo cuireaṽ amaċ ṗe na h-uġvarár, na
35 neiṫe a ṫa ann, aġur "vo ḃeanar ṗe rárpamuinṫ na

before Baptism, should be received into Favour otherwise than those who, being once delivered from the Bondage of Sin and the Devil, and endowed with the Gift of the Holy Ghost, had the Boldness to violate the Temple of God, and grieve the Holy Ghost.

VIII.   Thus far the Doctrine of the *Catholick Church*, assembled in Council, at *Trent ;* not in Regard of *scandalous* or openly wicked People, whom, besides all this, she orders to be put in *publick Penance*, at the Discretion of the *Ordinary :* Nor of obstinate Sinners, who, notwithstanding their repeated Promises of Restitution and Amendment of Life, do still persist in their sinful Practices and criminal Omissions of their Duty ; for, all these she excludes from the Participation of the Sacraments, until they give effectual Proofs of the Sincerity of their Repentance and Change of Conduct : But in Respect even of all those, who pass, in the Eyes of the World, for honest Men ; yet have, after coming to the Knowledge of Good and Evil, basely defiled that *interiour Purity and Beauty* they had received by the *Grace of Baptism.* And, that this Part of *her Doctrine*, on the Knowledge and due Execution whereof, the Salvation of almost all Men doth depend, may be *punctually* observed, and *well known of all ;* she, first, enjoins all Directors of Souls, to *impose Penances on their Penitents*, that shall be *suitable to the Quality of their Crimes, and to their Ability* or *Strength, least that by conniving at Sin, and by over-indulging their Penitents, they may be made Partakers of the Sins of Others.* Secondly, she requireth in thousand of Places, and particularly in that excellent *large Catechism* published by her Order, that *the Things*, therein contained, *concerning the Sacrament of Penance, and the several Parts thereof, should be so taught, that the Faithful may not only understand them* PERFECTLY,

Conc. Trid. Ses. 24, c. 8.

S. Car. Bor. Act. Part. 4. Instruct. Confess. Decr. of Pope In- noc. XI. March. 2. 1679.

Conc. Trid. ib. c. 8.

Catech. Conc. Trid. at the End of Penance.

C

Catech.
Conc.
Trid. de
Pænit.

1 " h-aıtṁıʒe, aʒuʃ ʃe ʒaċ ʃonn ʋı ʃa leıṫ, ʋo ṁúnaʋ aıʃ
" ċoʃ, naċ h-e aṁáın ʒo ʋ-cuıʒʃeaʋ na Cʃıoʃouıʒṫe ıaʋ ʒo
" ʋıonʒṁálca, aċc ʃóʃ ċum ʒo n-ʒlacʃaıʋíʃ ʃún ʋa ʃıʃıʋ,
" maılle ʃe ʒʃáʃaıʋ Ʋé, a ʒ-cuʃ a n-ʒníʋṁ ʒo cʃáıʋṫeaċ,
5 " ʋıaʒa."

IX.   A noıʃ ıʃ ʋeıṁın, naċ ʒaʋáıl ʒo ʃéıʒ ċaʃ an b-peacaʋ,
ná mıʃneaċ ċum a ʋeunca, an ceaʒaʒʒ-ʃo; ıʃ lúʒa ıoná
ʃın ʒo móʃ ıʃ ceaʋ peacaıʋ é; o aımʃıʒeaʃ ʃé ʃʃéaṁ an
uılc, eaʋon, ʃmuaıncıʒte coılceanaċa aʒuʃ mıanʒuʃa ʃéın
10 an peacaıʋ; aʒuʃ o ıʃ ʃollaʃaċ, ʒuʃ ab é ıʃ ʃéım ʋó,
" an cʃoıʋe ʋo cıṁċıll-ʒeaʃʃaʋ ıʃ an Spıoʃaʋ," aʒuʃ
an ʋuıne ʋo ʒlanaʋ caoʋ a ʃoıʒ; Ní, ann a b-ʃuıl ʒo
ʃunʃaʋaċ naoṁaʋ an Cʃıoʃouıʒe: o ca ʒo ʒ-cuıʃeann
ʋ'ualaċ aıʃ an b-peacaċ, caʃ éıʃ a ċoʒuaıʃ ʋo ṁıon-
15 ċuaʃcúʒaʋ ʒo ʋúṫʃaċcaċ, aʒuʃ caʃ éıʃ móʃáın ʃaocaıʃ
aʒuʃ ʋoʋʃoın, a ċıonca ʒo léıʃ ʋ'aʋṁáıl ʒo ʃıʃınneaċ,
ʋa ʒʃáıneaṁla aʒuʃ ʋa uaıʒnıʒe ıaʋ, ʋon bʃeıceaṁ ʋa
ʋ-caʒ Cʃıoʃo cúṁaċca peacaıʒe ʋo ṁaıceaʋ, no ʒan a
maıceaʋ, a n-aınım ʃéın, aʒuʃ ʃe n'uʒʋaʃáʃ; a léıʒıon
20 ċum na ʃácʃamuınceaʋ, no ʒan a léıʒıon; aʒuʃ bʃeaċ-
aıtṁıʒe ʋo ċuıʃ aıʃ, ʋo ʃéıʃ maʃ ıʃ ceaʃc, aʒuʃ ʋo ʃéıʃ
acʃuınne an ċıoncaıʒ: o ca ʒo ʒ-cuıʃeann ʋ'ʃıacaıʋ aıʃ
an aıtṁıʒeaċ an bʃeıceaṁnuʃ aıtʃıʒe, ʋo ċuıʃceaʃ aıʃ,
ċum a ṁıʒnıoṁ ʋo ʋıoʒaılc, aʒuʃ ċum a ʃmaċcaıʒte, no a
25 leıʒıʃ; aʒuʃ ċum ʒo ʋ-cıúbʃaʋ ʃe copċa buʋ h-ıomċuʋaıʋ
ʋo'n aıtʃıʒe uaʋ, ʋo ʒlacaʋ aıʃ ʃéın ʒo ʃonnṁaʃ, ċum a
ċoıṁlıonca ʒo ʃıʃınneaċ, ʃa ʃéın a beıṫ ʋíbeaʃca o na
ʃácʃamuıncıʋ, aʒuʃ ʃóʃ o ʃlaıcıoʃ Ʋé: o ca, ʃa ʋeoıʋ,
ʒo n-aıtnıʒeaʃ ʋo'n oıʋe ʃʃıoʃaʋálca a ʋualʒaʃ ʋo
30 ċóıṁlıonaʋ ʒo beaċc, ʃa ċáın a beıṫ ʃonn-ʃáıʃceaċ aʒuʃ
cıoncaċ a ʒ-coıʃcıʋ ʋuıne oıle: Neıce ʒo léıʃ naċ n-
ʒlacann aon-ʃʒáıle Eaʒluıʃe oıle, ʋa b-ʃuıl ıʃ an Eóʃoıʃ,
ʃaocaʃ aıʃ bıċ na ʋ-cımċıoll; nı h-e ʃın aṁáın, aċc
cáınıʋ uıle na neıce-ʃı, aʒ ʃáʋ, ʒuʃ cuınʒ ċʃuaıʋ, aʒuʃ
35 luıʒe a ʃoeaċ aıʃ ʃaoıʃʃe an c-ʃoıʃʒéıl ıaʋ.   Aıʃ an

*but also, by the Help of God, they may resolve in very Deed,
to perform them devoutly and religiously.*

IX.　　Now surely, this is not to *connive at, nor encourage Sin ;*
much less to give *Leave to sin,* since it strikes at the *very
Root,* thereof; at the *very deliberate Thought and Desire of
Sinning ;* and that it manifestly tends to the *Circumcision*　Rom. 2.
of the Heart in Spirit, to the purifying of the *inward Man,* 29. Ephes. 3.
wherein the Sanctity of a *Christian* doth *chiefly* consist; 16, &c.
Since it requires, that the Sinner, after a strict Examination, and after much Labour and Sorrow, should in the
Bitterness of his Soul, sincerely confess all his Offences, be
they never so foul, or never so secret, to the Judge estab-
lished by *Christ,* to remit or retain Sins, in *his Name, and
by his Authority ;* to admit him to the *Sacraments,* or refuse
him Admittance; and to inflict a Punishment upon him,
according to Equity, and the Dispositions of the Offender :
Since it obliges the Penitent to accept *freely,* and *sincerely*
undergo the Penance enjoined him both for his Punishment and Correction or Cure; and to *bring forth Fruits,
worthy of Penance,* under Pain of being excluded from the
Sacraments, and from the *Kingdom of God too :* Since,
lastly, the *Spiritual Director* is hereby ordered to be exact
in the Discharge of his Duty, under Pain of being accessory
to, and *guilty of the Sins of Another ;* which no other Kind
of *Church* in *Europe,* takes any Pains about; nay they all
censure it as *too severe,* and an Encroachment upon *Gospel-
Liberty.* It is then very uncharitable, and even very un-
fair to charge the *Church* with *giving Leave to offend God,*
on Account of the Misbehaviour of some *Particulars,* who
lie under great Hardships and Disadvantages, in Point of
Education and seasonable Instruction; or may be of as
perverse an Untowardness as a *Judas* among the twelve

C 2

1 ασὐδαṛ-ṛο, ιṛ ṛό ṁιοċαṛṫαnnαċ, ασυṛ ṛόṛ ιṛ ṛο éισceαṛṫ
α ċυṛ α leiṫ nα h-Ɛασluιṛe, σο υ-ṫυσαnn ṛí ceαυ υο ċάċ
υλιξεαὐ Ὀé υο ḃṛιṛeαὐ, ṛα ὐṛοιċιοmċαṛ beαξάιn υο
ὐαοιnιḃ άιṛιξe, α ṫα ṛαοι ṁόṛάn leαṫṛοιm ασυṛ ṁιοċοṁ-
5 σαιṛ υο ṫαοḃ οιυιṛ ασυṛ ṫeασαιṛξ ṫṛάṫαṁυιl ; nο υο
ṫeιξeοṁαὐ α ḃeιṫ υοṁύιnṫe, υṛοιċṁeιneαċ, mαṛ luυαṛ α
meαṛξ αn υά αḃṛοοl υeυξ. Ιṛ υeιṁιn nαċ luξα ιṛ
eυξċόṛαιξ é ιοnά αn αιṫιṛ úυ, υο ḃeιṛιυιṛ υιṫ-ċṛeιοṁeαċα
α n-αllόυ υο Ὀhια ṛéιn, ṛα ċιοnṫα α ṛοbυιl ṫοξṫα, nοċ
10 υο ṫυξ ṛοcαιṛ σο meιnιc υο nαιṁοιḃ Ὀé, α αιnm nαοṁṫα
υο ṁαṛluξαὐ ασυṛ υο ċάιneαὐ.

X. Σιὐeαὐ, nι h-ι αn ṁιοċlu-ṛο, α ḃeαṛṫαṛ υο'n Ɛασluιṛ,
ιṛ mό υο ξοιlleαṛ οιṛṫe ; αċṫ cαιlleαṁυιn nα beαṫα
ṛιοṛṛυιὐe υ'αnṁόṛάn υα cloιnn ṁιοὐύṫċυιṛυιξ, ασυṛ αn
15 ṫοιṛmeαṛξ υο ċυιṛιυ σο lαeṫeαṁυιl, ṫṛé nα m-beαṫα
οιlḃéιmιξ, αιṛ leαṫnύξαὐ αn ċṛeιυιṁ ṛíṛιnnιξ. Ασυṛ nί
h-e αn ṫṛυαιlleαὐ lοṁnοċṫ-ṛα nα m-béαṛ αn ṫ-αοn-οιc
αṁάιn, ṛόṛαṛ σο mοṛṁόṛ ο eαṛḃυιὐ ṫeασυιṛξ ασυṛ
υeαξοιυιṛ αnn αοιṛ nα h-όιξe : Cαιllṫeαṛ nα mίlṫe, nαċ
20 meαṛυιυ ċάċ ḃeιṫ lοċṫαċ, ṛα ḃeιṫ αn αιnḃṛιοṛ α n-
υυαιξαιṛ, ṫṛé nα σ-coιṛ ṛéιn : ιṛ ṛο ṁιnιc υο ḃíο υαοιne
όξα, υάṛ mό eυξαṛ ṛοιṁ αοιṛ α ḃ-ṛιċċιο bliαὐαιn ιοnά
υο'n ċιneαὐ υαοnnα σο h-ιοmlάn nα ὐιαὐ ṛιn, ṛάιṫṫe σο
υοṁυιn, ο'n σ-ceυυ αm αṛ ṫοṛυιξeαυαṛ υṛοċċlαοnṫα α
25 n-σeιneαṁnα αιṛ ḃοṛṛαὐ ṛυαṛ, α mοṛάn υο ṛeαcαιυιḃ
ṛοlυιξṫe nάṁαυυιṛ, ṫnύιṫ, υṛύιṛe, υιοξαlṫυιṛ, bαοιṛ, leιṛξe,
etc. ασυṛ coṁnυιξιο ιοnṫα υ'eαṛḃυιὐ οιυιṛ ασυṛ αιṛe
ṫṛάṫαṁυιl, (ᵃ) σο ḃ-ṛυαυαιξeαnn bάṛ αnαṛυιὐ αιṛ ṛιúbαl
α n-υιοξαlṫαṛ α mιξnιοṁ : "(ᵇ)α ṫάιυ ceυυṛαὐ ασυṛ
30 " ṛmυαιneαὐ ċṛοιὐe αn υυιne, clαοn ċυm οιlc ο αοιṛ nα
" h-όιξe ;" ασυṛ nι σnάṫαċ σο υ-ṫeιṛeαnn αιṛ αn σ-claοnαὐ
υṛċόιυeαċ-ṛα, υο ḃíοṛ αιṛ nα ḃṛοṛουξαὐ ασυṛ αιṛ nα
ξṛιοṛύξαὐ le ṫυιle ὐάṛαċṫαιξ αn ὐṛοċṛοmḃlα, αn ṫ-αοṛ-όξ
αιḃṛιοṛξ, ḃάιṛṛ-eυυṫṛοm υο ṫeιlξeαn α n-υιαιὐ α σ-cιnn
35 α m-beαlαċ α m-bαṛξαιὐċe, ṛυιl ṛόṛ υο ṛάṛυιξιυ ṛíṫċe

ᵃ Job. 15.
32, 33.
Prov. 10.
25, 27.
Eccle. 7.
18. v. 8.
c. 13. v.
ᵇ Gen. 8.
2:.

Apostles. It is, indeed, as unjust a Reproach as that made by *Unbelievers of old*, to *God himself*, on Account of the *Is. 52. 5.* Prevarications of his *chosen People*, who often gave Occasion *Ezech. 36. 20,* to the *Gentils* to prophane and *blaspheme* his *Holy Name.* [21, 22, 23.]

x.   But this Aspersion cast upon the Church, is not what *Rom. 2.* [24.] she most bewails; no, it is the Loss of the Salvation of so many degenerate Children; and the Obstacle they daily put, by their scandalous Lives, to the Propagation of the *Orthodox Faith.* Neither is this bare-faced Corruption of Manners, the only Evil that springs principally from the Want of Instruction, and a virtuous Education during Youth: Millions, who pass not, in the Eyes of the World for wicked Livers, are lost through a criminal Ignorance of their Duty: Young People, whereof more die before the Age of twenty, than of all Mankind after, are very often deeply engaged, since first the in-bred Corruption of Nature began to spring out, in many secret Sins of Malice, Envy, Impurity, Revenge, Vanity, Sloth, &c. and remain therein, for Want of seasonable Instruction and Care, until an * untimely Death snatches them away, in Punish- **Job. 15.* ment of their Transgressions: *The Sense and Thought of* *[32.] *Prov. 10.* *Man's Heart are prone to Evil from their Youth ;* and this *27. Eccle. 7.* sad Proneness to Sin, encouraged and excited by the *18. v. 8.* Torrent of bad Example, seldom or never fails to cast *c. 13. v. * Gen. 8.* slippery and unthinking Youth head-long into great *[2r.]* Disorders, even before the Age of twenty, when this Bosom Enemy is not diligently watched and restrained by early Instruction and Correction. Or if such as are

ı blıᴀóᴀın, ᴀn cᴀn nᴀċ b-ᚱᴀıᵽċeᴀᴩ ᚎo ᴅúcᴩᴀċcᴀċ, ᴀᚎuᴩ nᴀċ
ᚎ-coıᴩᚎceᴀᴩ ᚎo moċ ᴀ nᴀṁuıᴅ ċnıᴩe-ᴩı, ᴩe ceᴀᚎᴀᴩᚎ ᴀᚎuᴩ
ᴩmᴀċcuᚎᴀᴅ oıᴩeᴀṁnᴀċ. Πó mᴀ ċeᴀᚎṁᴀnn ᴅo'n ċuıᴅ ᴅóıᴅ
ᴩᴀᚎcᴀᴩ, beᴀᚎnᴀċ ᚎo léıᴩ, ᴀıᴩ láıṁ nᴀ nᴀṁᴀᴅ mıllcıᚎe-ᴩı
5 ᴅo ᴩuᚎᴀᴅ leo, ᵽıċċe blıᴀóᴀın ᴅo ᴩóᴩuᚎᴀᴅ, coᴩuıᚎıᴅ ᚎo
coıcċıonn ᴀnn ᴩın, ᴀıᴩ beıċ cᴩeᴀᴩᴀıcᴀ ᚎo léıᴩ ᴩe ᚎnoċuıᚎıᴅ
nᴀ beᴀċᴀ boıċce-ᴩı, ᴀᚎuᴩ ᴀıᴩ beıċ ᴅá líonᴀᴅ ᴩéın ᴩe
ᴩᴀoᴅnóᴩᴀıᴅ ᴀn c-ᴩᴀoᚎuıl-ᴩe : Πı cuıbe leo, cᴩe uᴀbᴀᴩ, ᴀn
ceᴀᚎᴀᴩᚎ Cᴩıoᴩᴏuıᚎe ᴅ'ᴩoᚎluım, ᚎıᴅ ᚎuᴩ ᴀb é ıᴩ ᴅuᴀlᚎᴀᴩ
10 ᴅo'n uıle neᴀċ cᴀ n'uıᴩeᴀᴩbuıᴅ, bıᴏᴅ ᚎuᴩ ᴩıᚎ no óᴩo-
ᵽlᴀıċ é : Πı mó ᴩóᴩ ᴀ cáıᴏ ᴀ ᚎ-cᴩuċ, ᴩoᴩᴀᴩ ᴅo buᴀın ᴀᴩ
ᴩeᴀnmóıᴩ no coṁᴩᴀᴅ ᴩᴀᴅᴀ ᴩoᚎlumcᴀ, mᴀ ċeᴀᚎṁᴀnn ᴅóıᴅ
ᴀ ᴩᴀṁuıl ᴅ'éıᴩᴅeᴀċċ, ᴅo ᴅıoᚎᴅáıl ᴅeᴀᚎᴏıᴏıᴩ ᴀᚎuᴩ blᴀıᴩ
ᴅ'ᴩᴀᚎᴀıl ᴀ ᴩıᴀṁ ᴀıᴩ neıcıᴅ ᴅıᴀᚎᴀ, no ᴩᴩıoᴩᴀᴅáıcᴀ : cᴀlcuıᴅ
15 ᴀnn ᴩnᴀ ᴅᴩoıċċleᴀċcᴀᴅᴀıᴅ ᴅo ċuᚎᴀᴅᴀᴩ ceᴀnᴀ ᴅóıᴅ ᴩéın ;
ᴀᚎuᴩ ᴩluıᚎıᴅ ᚎo coıcċıonn ᚎᴀċ ní, ᴅo ᴩᴀᴩuıᚎeᴀᴩ ᴀ n-ᴀn-
ṁıᴀnᴀ ᴀnċuṁᴀċcᴀċᴀ, no ṁeuᴅuıᚎeᴀᴩ ᴀ mᴀoın ᴩᴀoᚎᴀıcᴀ ;
ᴀıᴩ ċoᴩı, ᚎo ᴅ-céıᚎıᴅ nᴀ ᴅᴩoċnóᴩᴀ-ᴩo ᴀ b-ᴩᴩéıṁ coṁᴅoṁᴀın
ᴩın ıᴩ ᴀn ᴀnᴀm, ᚎuᴩ le ᴩáᴩᴩᴀᴏcᴀᴩ, le coṁᴩᴀc, ᴀᚎuᴩ le
20 mıoᴩbuılıᴅ ᴩollᴀᴩᴀċᴀ ᚎᴩáᴩ ᴅé ᴀṁáın, ıᴩ ᴩéıᴏıᴩ buᴀıᴅ
ᴅo bᴩeıċ oᴩċᴀ : Πeıċe ᴅ'ᴩıonn ᚎo léıᴩ ᴀn Πᴀoṁ oıᴩᴅeıᴩc
ᴀıbıᴩcın ıonn ᴀ ċolᴀınn ᴩéın, ᴀṁuıl mᴀᴩ ᴩoıllᴩıᚎeᴀᴩ ᴩe
óᴩ ᴀıᴩᴏ ᴅo'n ᴅóṁᴀn, ᴀ leᴀbᴀᴩ nᴀ n-ᴀᴏṁálᴀċ ; ᴀᚎuᴩ nı
h-eᴀᚎuıl ᴩıᴩ ᴀ ᴩáᴅ "ᚎo b-ᴩáᴩᴀıᴅ ᴅᴩoıċṁıᴀncᴀ o ᴀncoıl,

Lib. 8. 25 "ᴀᚎuᴩ ᚎo b-ᴩᴀᴩánn cleᴀċcᴀᴅ o nᴀ ᴅᴩoıċṁıᴀnᴀıᴅ, ᴀn
Conf. c. 5. "cᴀn nᴀċ ᚎ-cuıᴩceᴀᴩ ᴩᴩıᴀn leo, ᴀᚎuᴩ ᴩıᴀċcᴀnuᴩ o'n
"ᚎ-cleᴀċcᴀᴅ nᴀċ ᚎ-coıᴩᚎceᴀᴩ."

XI.   So mᴀᴩ níᴏ nᴀ cᴩí nᴀıṁᴅe ᴩeᴀn-ᴩᴀlcᴀnᴀċᴀ-ᴩo ᴀn
ᴀnmᴀ, eᴀᴅon, ᴀn ċolᴀnn, ᴀn ᴩᴀoᚎᴀl, ᴀᚎuᴩ ᴀn ᴅıᴀbᴀl,
30 coıṁċeᴀnᚎᴀl, mᴀᴩ ᴅéᴀᴩcᴀ, ᴀᚎuᴩ conᴩᴀᴅ ceılᚎe ᴩe ċéıle,
ċum nᴀ n-óᚎ, ᴀᚎuᴩ ᴀn cıneᴀᴅ ᴅᴀᴏnnᴀ ᚎo h·ıomlán ᴅo ᴅıċ-
ċeᴀnnuᚎᴀᴅ ᴀ m-boᴩᴩᴀᴅ ᴀᚎuᴩ ᴀ m-blác nᴀ h-óıᚎe : So mᴀᴩ
cıomáınceᴀᴩ ᴩıᴩ nᴀ cᴩí nᴀıṁᴅıᴅ ᴅıoċoıᴩᚎıce-ᴩe ᴀn ċuıᴅ ıᴩ
mó ᴅo'n ᴀoᴩ-óᚎ, nᴀ ᴩuᴀcᴀᴩ ċum ᴀ n-ᴀıṁleıᴩ : So mᴀᴩ ċᴩéıᚎıᴅ
35 ᴅıᴀ, ᴀn cᴀn buᴅ ᴩıᴀċcᴀnᴀċ ᴅóıᴅ coᴩuᚎᴀᴅ ᴀıᴩ ᴀ ṁᴀᴩ :
So mᴀᴩ ᴀ cáıᴏ ᴀn ᴀınbᴩıoᴩ, no ᴀ n-ᴅeᴀᴩmᴀᴅ ᴅıombuıᴅeᴀċ

almost left a Prey to this in-born and most dangerous
Foe, happen to outlive that Number of Years, they then,
commonly, begin to be taken up wholly with the Affairs
of this miserable Life, and to be filled with the Maxims or
Customs of the World : They proudly scorn to be *catechized*,
although it is the Duty of every one, that stands in Need
of it, were he a King or Prince : Neither are they in a
Disposition to profit of Sermons, or long and learned
Discourses, if they chance to assist at any such, for Want
of good Principles, and of ever having had a Taste for
pious or spiritual Things : They harden in the evil Habits,
they have already contracted, and generally stop not at
any Thing, that will gratify their Predominant Passions,
or advance their worldly Interest : So that these vicious
Customs take such a deep Root in the Soul, that it is with
incredibile Pains and Combats, and by a manifest Miracle
of the Divine Grace, they can be rooted out : Such is
the great Force of bad Habits, contracted in Youth, and
encreased with Age. All which the great S. *Augustin*
experienced in his own Person, as he openly declares to
the World, in his Book of Confessions ; and is not afraid
to say, that *from a depraved Will proceed evil Desires ;*   *Lib. 8.*
when evil Desires are indulged, they become a Custom ; and *Conf. c. 5.*
a Custom, not resisted, becomes a Necessity.

XI.   Thus the three *inveterate Enemies* of the Soul, the
Flesh, the *World*, and the *Devil*, do combine, as it were,
and conspire to the Destruction of young People, and of
all Mankind in the Bloom or Flower of their Age. Thus
the greatest Part of Youth, hurryed along to Destruction by
these three implacable Enemies, abandon God, when they
should begin to serve him ; and either are ignorant of, or

1 na n-ᵹeallaṁun, vo ċuᵹavaɼ óɼ áɼvo uaċa, an can vo
ᵹlacavaɼ baiɼveav; aᵹuɼ na c-cíovlaiceavav voiṁeaɼva,
vo ɼuaɼavaɼ o ṁaiċeaɼ voċoimɼiᵹċe an Coiṁve: noċ
iɼ uɼcóiv coicċionn, ɼa aɼ cóiɼ vo ᵹać Cɼíoɼuiᵹe maiċ
5 bɼiɼeav amaċ anɼna bɼiaċɼaiḃ-ɼe h-1eɼemiaɼ, an ɼáiv:
"uċ naċ uiɼᵹeava mo ċeann, aᵹuɼ naċ ḃ-ɼuil cobuɼ veóɼ

Jer. 9. 1.
"1onn mo ɼúiliḃ, čoɼ ᵹo n-ᵹuilɼinn vo ló aᵹuɼ v'oívce
"ɼa ṽíċceannav člainne mo ṁuinciɼe." Oíɼ iɼ maɼ ɼo
cɼuailliᵹċeaɼ aᵹuɼ eaɼmuilceaɼ ɼe h-ainḃɼioɼ aᵹuɼ ɼe
10 ɼeacav an čuiv iɼ neiṁcioncuiᵹe v'aɼ n-aoiɼ, aᵹuɼ an
ɼoinn iɼ áille v'Eaᵹluiɼ Ṽé, vɼeaɼ cɼé ɼailliᵹe, no ainᵏ
ḃɼioɼ aᵹuɼ neaṁċɼáḃav an acaɼ aᵹuɼ na máċaɼ, noċ vo
beiɼ ᵹo coicċionn v'a n-aiɼe aṁáin, a ᵹ-clann vo ċabaiɼc
ɼuaɼ a m-baoɼ, a m-báɼɼ-ᵹlóɼ aᵹuɼ a n-ᵹɼáv neiceav cal-
15 ṁuiᵹe: vɼeaɼ cɼe eaɼḃuiv veaᵹoiviᵹeav ɼoᵹluma, no
veaᵹṽaoineav oile va'ɼ ᵹnocuiᵹe, a n-aimɼiɼ aᵹuɼ a
ɼaocaɼ vo čaiceav ᵹo ceaɼ-ᵹɼávaċ ɼe h-eóluɼ na beaċa
ɼioɼɼuiṽe vo ċabaiɼc vo'n aoɼ-óᵹ: vɼeaɼ cɼé cionca na
leanaḃ ɼéin; óiɼ ní móɼ a m-beann aiɼ oiveaɼ, aᵹuɼ ɼóɼ
20 iɼ minic vo ċeiciv uav, an ṁéiv iɼ ɼéiviɼ leo, cum iav
ɼéin vo ṁilleav ᵹo bɼáċaċ: vɼeaɼ ɼóɼ cɼé uiɼeaɼbaiv
leabɼán n-viaᵹa, aɼ aɼ ḃɼéiviɼ a v-ceaᵹaɼᵹ aᵹuɼ a
ᵹ-ceaɼav čum caon-ṽúċɼacča, čoṁluaċ aᵹuɼ ḃiv ioɼṁúince,
aᵹuɼ a ᵹ-cɼuċ blaiɼ v'ɼáᵹail aiɼ neiċiḃ neaṁṽa: oíɼ, maɼ

Prov. 22. 6.
25 veiɼ an Spioɼav Naoṁ, "An leanaḃ cabaɼċaɼ ɼuaɼ ann
ɼa m-bealač ann aɼ cóiɼ ṽó ɼiúbal, an can ɼéin biaɼ
áɼɼuiv, ní imeoċaiv ɼé aɼ." Veiɼ maɼ an ᵹ-ceuvna an

Eccli. 6. 18.
1onav oile: "A ṁic, ᵹlac ceaᵹaɼᵹ o v'óiᵹe, aᵹuɼ vo
"ᵹeabaiɼ eaᵹna ᵹo veiɼeav vo ɼaoᵹuil."

XII. 30 Iɼ e móɼ-ᵹoncanuɼ na v-ceaᵹaɼᵹ Cɼíoɼuiᵹe leiceavača
vo ɼᵹaɼavaɼ amaċ bɼáiċɼe ɼaoċɼača, ɼoᵹlumča oiɼv
San-Fɼoinɼiaɼ a loḃan, cuilleav aiɼ čeuv bliavain o
ɼoin; aᵹuɼ ᵹéiɼ-ḃɼeacnuᵹav na móɼ-oilc ɼáɼaɼ o ainḃɼioɼ,
vɼeaɼ cɼé eaɼḃuiv leabɼán oiviɼ; maɼaon ɼe mian móɼ
35 cuiviúᵹav éiᵹin vo ċabaiɼc ɼe h-aoɼ-óᵹ leaċcɼiomaċ na

ungratefully forget the solemn Promise, they made him at the Font of Baptism ; and the inestimable Favours, they have received from his infinite Goodness ; which is such a *publick Calamity* as ought to move every *good Christian* to utter these Expressions of the Prophet *Jeremy : Oh, that* Jer. 9. 1. *my Head were full of Water, and mine Eyes had a Fountain of Tears, that I might weep Day and Night, for the Desolation of the Children of my People.* For, thus, the most innocent Age of Life, the fairest Portion of God's Church, is cor-rupted and dishonoured by Ignorance and Sin, partly through either the Negligence, or Ignorance and Impiety of Parents, who commonly bestow all their Care in educa-ting their Children in Vanity, and in the Love of earthly Goods: Partly for Want of virtuous and well-instructed School-Masters or Catechists, who would zealously employ their Time and Labour in making Youth understand the Science of Salvation: Partly through the Fault of Children themselves, who little care for Instruction, and often shun it, all they can, to their own eternal Ruin: And partly also for Want of little pious Books, whereby they may be instructed, and formed to Devotion as soon as they are teachable and capable of receiving pious Impressions; for as the Holy Ghost saith, *A Child trained up in the Way he should* Prov. 22. *go, shall not, even when he is old, depart from it.* He saith 6. also in another Place : *Son, receive Instructions from your* 1 Ecc. 8. *Youth, and you shall find Wisdom to the End of your Life.*

XII. It is the great Scarcity of those large *Irish Catechisms,* published upwards of an hundred Years ago, by the laborious and learned *Franciscans* of *Lovain ;* and the Consideration of those great Evils, which arise from Ignorance, partly for Want of instructive Books ; together with a great Desire of contributing to the Instruction of

1 h-Éιριοnn το τeᴀҕᴀrҕ, το ċuιrmιҕ ᴀn Ceᴀҕᴀrҕ Críoroυιҕe-
rι, nᴀrι n-τιᴀιὁ; ᴀnn ᴀ mínιҕċeᴀrι nᴀ h-ᴀιċeᴀnτᴀ, nᴀ
ráċrᴀmuιnτe, ᴀn urɴᴀιҕ, etc., níor rοιρleιċne ιοnᴀ ᴀnn
ᴀοιn-τeᴀҕᴀrҕ Críoroυιҕe ҕᴀοιὁeιlҕe, ná bréιτιρ béᴀρlᴀ,
5 τᴀρ cuιρeᴀὁ ᴀ ҕ-clόὁ ҕο nuιҕe ro: Aҕur τρé ᴀrι réιτιρ το
ὁοιnιὁ όҕᴀ, ᴀҕur árruιҕe réιn, rοҕluιm ᴀ m-beᴀċᴀ, mᴀιlle

1. S. Pet. 3. 15.

re ҕráҕᴀιὁ Τé, το ċᴀιċeᴀὁ ҕο Críorοᴀṁuιl, ᴀҕur ᴀ beιċ
ullᴀṁ το ҕnáċ re ráҕᴀṁ éιҕιn το ċᴀbᴀιρτ το ҕᴀċ ᴀοn, το
rireᴀr οrċᴀ ᴀὁὁᴀr nᴀ muιnιҕιne ᴀ τᴀ ᴀcᴀ.

XIII. 10

10 Τo rιnneᴀὁ τιċċιοll ᴀιρ rοclᴀιὁ cοιṁιὁτeᴀċᴀ το reᴀċ-
nᴀὁ, leᴀċ-ᴀmuιҕ ᴀṁáιn το'n ċuιο τιοὁ το τuҕ ᴀn cρeιτeᴀṁ
ᴀ roeᴀċ, ᴀҕur το τίrlιҕeᴀὁ ὁό. Ιr ι ᴀn ҕᴀοιὁeιlҕ ιr
rοċuιҕrιҕċe, ᴀҕur ιr cοιċċιnne το cuιρeᴀὁ ríor ᴀnn, ᴀҕ

S. Aug. in Ps. 138.

brιeιċ το roҕuιn, ᴀιρ lοrҕ Αιbιρτιn Ɲᴀοṁċᴀ, ὁιοṁοlᴀὁ nᴀ
15 n-eοlҕᴀċ τ'rulᴀnҕ, τᴀρ ᴀ beιċ τορċᴀ ᴀιρ ċᴀċ. Cuҕᴀὁ
rόr ᴀιρe le cορρ-rοcᴀιl, nᴀċ ὁ-ruιl cοιċċιοnn ᴀ m-beᴀҕán
το ṁιοn-rᴀnnᴀιὁ το'n ríοҕᴀċτ, το ṁínιúҕᴀὁ: Αҕ rο ᴀ
ҕ-cοṁᴀrτᴀ, (¹) etc. nοċ το ҕeιὁċeᴀr rοιṁ nᴀ rοcᴀιl, το
ṁínιҕeᴀr ιᴀτ, ᴀ n-τeιρeᴀὁ nᴀ n-τuιlleοҕ. Το ċᴀοὁ nᴀ
20 cοτᴀ ὁe, ᴀ τᴀ m-béᴀρlᴀ, ιr ᴀιρ rτᴀrmuᴀιneᴀὁ το τᴀρρuιnҕ-
eᴀὁ í ҕο rο beᴀċċ ᴀr ᴀn n-ҕᴀοιὁeιlҕ, mᴀr ҕeᴀll ᴀιρ ᴀn
τρeᴀm το lᴀὁrᴀr béᴀρlᴀ ᴀṁáιn. Το meᴀrᴀὁ nᴀċ ᴀρ beᴀҕ
nᴀ h-áιτe τοn Sҕρίbιnn Τhιᴀҕᴀ, etc., ᴀr ᴀρ τιοmρuιҕeᴀὁ
ᴀn τeᴀҕᴀrҕ-rο, το ċuρ ríor ᴀnn ᴀοιn-τeᴀnҕᴀιὁ, το brίҕ
25 ҕο ҕ-cοιṁrieᴀҕrᴀιο rιοrruιҕċe ᴀҕur rreᴀҕᴀρċᴀ ᴀn τá
ċeᴀnҕċᴀ ҕο cοṁċροm re ċéιle: Ιr léοr mᴀρ leιċ-rҕéᴀl
ᴀιρ ron lοċċ nᴀ τ-τeᴀnҕċᴀὁ ᴀҕur ᴀn clόὁᴀ, ιmċeᴀċċ ᴀn
τιοmρuιҕċeόρᴀ ᴀr ᴀ h-τίρ ὁúċċᴀιr, τuιlleᴀὁ re blιᴀὁᴀιn
ᴀιρ ċρίοċᴀτ ο roιn, ᴀҕur τuὁ-ᴀιnὁrιοr ᴀn clόὁᴀτόρᴀ ná'ρι
30 ċuιҕ ᴀοn rοcᴀl ᴀṁáιn το ċeᴀċċᴀr το'n τá ċeᴀnҕᴀιὁ. Ο ιr
ιοnᴀnn réιm nο eᴀҕᴀr το'n τeᴀҕᴀrҕ-rο ᴀҕur το h-τeᴀҕᴀrҕ
Críoroυιҕe Chοṁᴀιrle h-Cρenτ; ᴀҕur ο'r ᴀr ᴀn Sҕρίbιnn
Τhιᴀҕᴀ, ᴀr leᴀὁρᴀιὁ nᴀ n-Αιċρeᴀċ Ɲᴀοṁċᴀ, ᴀҕur ᴀr rᴀnᴀ-
ráɴᴀιὁ nᴀ h-Eᴀҕluιre το cruιnnιҕeᴀὁ ᴀ ὁunúὁᴀr, ní cόιρ
35 ᴀ ṁeᴀr, ҕur re τuιne ᴀιnneιρeᴀċ, ᴀċτ re Τιᴀ réιn, ᴀҕur
re nᴀ h-reᴀριὁrόҕᴀnτuιҕιὁ τοҕċᴀ το h-οιbριҕeᴀὁ e.

the poor *Irish* Youth; that gave Birth to the following
Irish Catechism: Wherein the Commandments, Sacraments, Prayers, &c. are treated more at Large than in any
Irish, or perhaps, *English Catechism*, that hitherto appeared
in Print: And whereby young People, and even those of
riper Years may learn, through the Grace of God, to live
Christian-like; and *be always ready to give some Satisfaction* 1 S. *Pet.*
to every one, that asketh them a Reason of that Hope, which is 3. 15.
in them.

XIII.   Endeavours were made to avoid foreign Expressions,
save only such, as Religion had introduced, and are con-
secrated to it.   The plainest and most obvious *Irish* is
used therein, preferring, after the Example of S. Augustin, *In Ps.*
rather to be censured by Grammarians than misunderstood of 138.
the People.   Care also was taken to explain certain Words,
which are not used in some Cantons of the Kingdom; and
are marked thus (1), &c.   And the Words that explain
them, are set down at the Bottom of the Pages, with the
like Mark.   As to the *English* Part thereof, it was translated, upon a second Thought, perhaps too litterally, from
the *Irish*, in Favour of those, who speak only English.
It was thought needless to point out, but in one Language,
the Places of Scripture &c. from which this Doctrine is
drawn; since the Questions and Answers of both Languages do exactly correspond.   An Absence of upwards of
31. Years from one's native Country, and the profound
ignorance of the Printer, who understood not one Word of
either Language, will be a sufficient Apology, for the Faults
of both the Languages, and the Press.   As the Method or
Order of the Work, is the same with that of the *Catechism*
of the Council of *Trent*, and the Matter thereof is chiefly
taken out of the *sacred Scripture*, the Writings of the
holy Fathers, and Decisions of the *Church*, it ought not to
be considered as the Work of a miserable Man, but of *God*
himself, and his *chosen Servants.*

XIV. 1 Iaꞃᴄaꞃ ᵹo ᴠúᴛꞃaᴄᴛaᴄ́ maꞃ aᴄ́ᴄuinᵹe aiꞃ ᵹaᴄ́ aon ᴠ'ó
ꞃaᴄ́aiᴠ ꞃe a ᴠ-ᴄaiꞃᵬe, ᵹuiᴠe le ᴠuine uaꞃal ꞃáiꞃṁeaꞃaṁuil,
eaᴠon, ᑭhilip Ioꞃeᵽ ᵽeꞃꞃoᴄ, ᴄꞃ̇ᵹeaꞃna ṁanéiꞃ ᵬaꞃꞃmon
aᵹuꞃ ᴠúiᴛᴄ́iᴠeaᴠ oile, ꞃ́ioꞃe ᴠ'Oꞃᴠ ꞃ́ioᵹa ꞃ́laoiṁ ṁiᴄ́il,
5 etc. le aꞃ ab ionṁuin ᴄlanna ᵹaoiᴠeal ꞃe ꞃeal ꞃaᴠa, aᵹuꞃ
o ᵬ-ꞃuaꞃaᴠaꞃ ᵹo miniᴄ móꞃán ᴠioᵬ coṁaꞃᴛaiᴠe ceana :
aᵹuꞃ ᵹan a ᴄoṅᵹnaṁ ni ᴄiucꞃaᴠ an mion-ꞃaoᴛaꞃ-ꞃ̇o ᴄóiᴠᴄe
ᴄum an ᴄ·ꞃoluiꞃ. a ᴄa muiniᵹin aᵹ an ᵬ-ꞃeaꞃ ᴠioluma, ᵹo
ᴠ-ᴄaiꞃᵬeáṅꞃuiᴠᴄeaꞃ an muinᴄiꞃᴠeaꞃ céaᴠna ᴠó ꞃéin : Oa
10 ᴄ́aoᵬ-ꞃan ᴠe, ni ᴠeuna ꞃailliᴠe, a ᴄꞃoiᴠe ᴠ'aꞃᴠuᵹaᴠ ᵹo
laeᴄeaṁuil ᴄum na ᵬ-ꞃlaiᴛioꞃ, aᵹ ꞃꞃim ᵹo h-oiꞃ́iꞃeal aiꞃ
Ohia, aᴄaiꞃ na huile ᴛꞃóᴄaiꞃe, ᵹan a ainneiꞃ ꞃéin ᴠo ᴄuꞃ
ᴄoiꞃꞃniꞃ̇ᵹ aiꞃ ᴄ́ioᴠlaiᴄiᴠiᵬ ꞃ́iᵹ na ꞃéile ; no ᴠo ᴄoꞃᵹ aiꞃ
an ᵬ-ꞃoiꞃᴄeaᴠal neaṁ́ᴠa-ꞃo na ᴄoꞃᴄa, iꞃ ᴠual ᴠó, ᴠo
15 ᴄ́aᵬaiꞃᴄ uaᴠ ann anmannaiᴠ ᴄ́áiᴄ́ : ᵹo maᴠ ᴄoil le aꞃ
ᵹ-ᴄꞃuᴄuiᵹᴄeóiꞃ, aᵹuꞃ le aꞃ ᵬ-ꞃuaꞃᵹuilᴄeóiꞃ ᴛꞃóᴄuiꞃeaᴄ́,
ᵬꞃiaᴄꞃa an leaᴠaiꞃ-ꞃe, eaᴠon, a ᴛeaᵹaꞃᵹ ᴠiaᵹa ꞃéin, ᴠo
ᵬeoᴠuᵹaᴠ ꞃe na Spioꞃaᴠ ꞃ́laoṁ, aᵹuꞃ ᴠo ᴄ́aᵬaiꞃᴄ aiꞃ an
ᴠꞃoinᵹ ᴠá'ꞃ ᴠealᵬaᴠ é, aᴠṁáil aiꞃ na léiᵹeaᴠ, no aiꞃ na
20 ᴄ́loꞃ ᴠóiᵬ, ᵹo ᵬ-ꞃuil ꞃé ᴠ-ualaᴄ́ ᴠoꞃᵹaoilᴄe oꞃᴄa, eiꞃion ᴠo
ꞃiaꞃ ; aᵹuꞃ a ᵬeiᴄ́ ᴠeaꞃᵬᴄa ᵹuꞃ ab é ᵹnoᴄuiᵹe a nanma
a naon-ᵹnoᴄuiᵹe, aᵹuꞃ an ᴛ-aon-áᴠᵬaꞃ ꞃá'ꞃ ᴄꞃuᴄuiᵹeaᴠ
iaᴠ ; ᵹo maᴠ áill ꞃiꞃ an Spioꞃaᴠ ꞃ́laoṁ laᵬaiꞃᴄ ꞃe na
ᵹ-ᴄꞃoiᴠᴄ́iᵬ, iꞃ an am ᵹ-ceuᴠna a léiᵹꞃiᴠ, no a ᵹ-ᴄloiꞃꞃiᴠ
25 na ᵬꞃiaᴄꞃa-ꞃo ; aᵹuꞃ a n-ᵹluaꞃaᴄᴄ ꞃe na ᵹꞃáꞃaiᵬ ᴄ́um an
eóluiꞃ neaṁ́ᴠa, ᴠo ᵹeaᴠaiᴠ ann, ᴠo ᴄuꞃ a n-ᵹnioṁ : ᵹo

S. Math.
18. 2, 3,
5, 6. vv.
19. c. 13,
14, 15. vv.
S. Marc.
10. 13, 14,
&c.

n-ᴠeonuiᵹe aꞃ ꞃ́lánuiᵹᴄeoiꞃ Ioꞃa ᴄꞃioꞃᴠ an ᴛeaꞃ-ᵹꞃáᴠ móꞃ,
ᴠo ᴄ́aiꞃᵬéin ꞃe ꞃéin ᵹo miniᴄ ᴠo ᴄaoᵬ ꞃláinᴄe ꞃ́oꞃꞃuiᴠe na
n-ᴠaoineaᴠ óᵹa, ᴠ'áiᴄ́ᵬeoᴠuᵹaᴠ a ᵹ-ᴄꞃoiᴠᴄ́iᵬ na n-uile,
30 ᴠá'ꞃ ᴠualᵹaꞃ a ᴠ-ᴛeaᵹaꞃᵹ aᵹuꞃ a ꞃmaᴄᴛuᵹaᴠ : aᵹuꞃ ᵹan
léiᵹean na h-anmanna, ᴠ'ꞃuaꞃᵹail ꞃe ꞃe na ꞃuil ṁóꞃ-luaiᵹ
ꞃéin, ᴠo ᴄáilleaᴠ, ná a ꞃulanᵹ ᴠóiᵬ " ꞃ́úᵬal, maꞃ ꞃ́úᵬlaiᴠ
"na ꞃáᵹánuiᵹ a m-baoꞃ a n-aiᵹniᴠ, aᵹá ᵬ-ꞃuil a ᴠ-ᴄuiᵹꞃe
"aiꞃ na ᴠallaᴠ ꞃe ᴠoꞃᴄaᴠuꞃ, aiꞃ na m-ᵬeiᴄ́ ᵹᵹaꞃᴄa o
35 "ᵬeaᴄ́a Oé, ᴠo ᵬꞃiᵹ an ainᵬꞃiꞃ a ᴄa ionnᴄa, ᴛꞃé ᴠall-
"ꞃaᴠaꞃᴄ a ᵹ-ᴄꞃoiᴠe."—Ephes. 4. 17, 18.

XIV.   Such as will reap any Advantage from it, are earnestly beseeched to pray for a very worthy Gentleman, *PHILIP-JOSEPH PERROT*, Lord of the Mannor of *BARMON*, and other Territories, Knight of the *Royal Order of S. Michael &c.* who, of a long Time, is well affected to the *Irish* Nation; and has often given Proofs of his Affection to several of them : And without whose Concurrence, this little Work would never come to Light. It is hoped, they will also grant the like Favour to the *Compiler*, who, on his Part, will not fail lifting up his Heart daily to Heaven, humbly beseeching God, the *Father of Mercies*, that his own Unworthiness may not stop the Effects of the *Divine Bounty*, nor hinder these heavenly Instructions from producing in Souls the Fruit, they ought to bring forth : That our merciful Maker and Redeemer may animate the Words of this Book, viz. His own Divine Instructions, with his holy Spirit; and cause them for whom it is made, to acknowledge in reading or hearing it, the strict Obligations they have to serve him, and to be persuaded, that the Affair of their Salvation, is their only Affair, and the sole End of their Creation : That the *Holy Ghost* may speak to their Hearts, at the same Time, that these Words inform their Eyes or Ears; and move them with his Grace to receive and practice the Precepts they shall find here for their Salvation : That our Divine Saviour may make that great Zeal, which he was pleased so often to manifest for the Salvation of Youth, revive in all those, whose Duty it is to instruct and correct young People: And that he may not let the Souls be lost, which he has redeemed with his most *precious Blood ;* nor permit them to *Walk as the Gentils walk in the Vanity of their Mind, having the Understanding covered with Darkness, alienated from the Life of God, through the Ignorance which is in them, because of the Blindness of their Heart.* Ephes. 4. 17. 18.

S. Mat. 18. 2, 3, 5, 6. vv. 19. c. 13, 14, 15.

S. Marc. 10. 13, 14, &c.

A certain latitude in spelling and accents, observable in the text, is explained by the following quotation from Donlevy's Appendix :—

1. " Note that the Irish, commonly, put an Accent over the Vowel that ought to be pronounced long, for Example, Cíoρ, Céιρ, Móρáη.

2. "That an u, immediately followed by ḃ (bh), ṗ (ṗh), ṡ, or ṁ, either in the Beginning of Words of two Syllables, or in the Middle of Words of three or more Syllables, is commonly long, and consequently needs no Accent. The same may be said of a single ι, going before ḃ, ṗ, or ṡ, as for Example, Uṡṗáρ, úṁal, bunúṗaρ, ρlíṡe, cρoíṫe.

3. "That, e, ι, o by themselves, as it often happens, are always long, and therefore need no Accent : The same may be said of the Particles ca, ρa, ρo, ṗa, ṡa, ṗa, ṡa, ρe, ρι, and of all Words of one Syllable, ending with a, e, ι, or u, as me, cρe, cρι, cu, la, &c., except ba (Cows), ṡa (a Dart, or Ray of Light, ṡać rather); except also a by it self, na when it signifies neither (nor) nor (than) ; and the Relatives ṗe ṗι, ṗe ṗι which are always short.

4. "That the broad Vowels do often stand for one another, when they are not long, nor have a full, clear and distinct Sound, especially in the Beginning and End of Words ; and so do the small Vowels e, ι, sometimes, serve for each other ; as for Instance, oιρρρoll, which may be as correctly wrote uιρρeall : Saoṡal, thus Saoṡul; aṁuιl, thus aṁaιl, &c."

For the elucidation of the text, I have been obliged to discuss briefly some grammatical questions on which

fresh light has been thrown in the texts, with glossary, published by Dr. Atkinson for the Royal Irish Academy; for example :—

Meaning of ιſ and ατάιm.

See ατάιm.

Relative tense and pronoun.

See α.

Irish infinitive and form το búαλατ.

See το.

In the Glossary I have called the present in ann the *Cons. pres.* Recent grammatical analysis (see Dr. Atkinson's Paper " On the Use of Two Inflexional Forms of the Verb in·Irish," in *Proceedings*, R. I. A., 3rd series, vol. I., No. 3, page 416) has shown that that tense has no consuetudinal force whatever, and that it is an enclitic present. However, as it is called in several grammars *Cons. pres.*, to avoid confusing the reader I have retained the term.

GLOSSARY.

ᴀ, *prep.*, in (ecl.), (Mid. Ir., i n-) govs. dat. Denotes, like the Latin *in*, 'rest' and 'motion.' Usually here written ᴀn before vowels. This prep., united with sing. def. art., forms here iſ ᴀn, the original *s* of the article being revived by the prep.: see ᴀn. 'In him,' ᴀnn, ıoıın-ſᴀn; 'in her,' ınnce; 'in them,' ıonncᴀ; 'in his,' ıonn ᴀ.

ᴀ, *a prefix prep.*, often separated here and by other writers from the word to which it belongs, v. g.—

ᴀ cᴀ *for* ᴀcᴀ.
ᴀ beıſceaſ ,, ᴀbeıſceaſ.
ᴀ ꝺeıſ ,, ᴀꝺeıſ.

ᴀ, used a few times here as equivalent to ꝺo before infin. Neilson gives the two forms ꝺo buᴀlᴀꝺ and ᴀ buᴀlᴀꝺ as identical in sense; but as the vowel ᴀ is much overtaxed in Mod. Ir., its use in this case is not to be recommended.

ᴀ, a form arising from the dismembering of the art. before vowels, thus:—
ᴀ nᴀnmᴀ, for ᴀn ᴀnmᴀ.

ᴀ, *poss. pronom. adj.* (1) his, its; (2) her, its; (3) their.

(1) Asp.; besides its use as an ordinary poss. pr., it has some idiomatic uses:—

   (A) For personal pronoun, him, it, where the object of a transitive infinitive is to be indicated, thus—To adore him, ꝺ'ᴀ ᴀꝺſᴀꝺ, not ꝺ'ᴀꝺſᴀꝺ é.

   (B) To call attention, by anticipation, to a coming clause, thus—ᴀcᴀ ᴀ ſıoſ ᴀᵹum ᵹo, &c., 'I know that,' &c.—literally, 'there is knowledge of it' (*i. e.* the facts about to be stated). Cf. the Latin habit of anticipating the coming phrase, v. g. 'I say that Caesar is the wisest of men,' Dico quod C. sit sapientissimus virorum; or with prolepsis, Id, dico quod, &c. Here ꝺᴀ ᵹneᴀmuᵹᴀꝺ ꝺıob ᴀ munᴀꝺ, 'enjoining on them it' (prol.) its teaching to the people'—i. e. 'enjoining on them its teaching to the people,' 'enjoining on them to teach it to the people.' To this proleptic use is reducible its use with the infin. after verbs of *thinking, saying,* &c. It serves to introduce the thought or the saying.

   (C) With *indecl. dem. pr.* ſın, ſo, wherever they would require, if declinable to be in the genitive case, v. g. 'When he had said this,' ᴀſ nᴀ ſᴀꝺ ſo ꝺó; 'in regard of this,' ꝺᴀ ċᴀob ſo. On the separation here between ᴀ and ſo, see def. art.

   (D) In composition with prep. ꝺo, before nouns, and adjectives in compar. degree, to intensify those parts of speech, v. g. ꝺᴀ ṁéıꝺ, 'of whatever size it be'; here ꝺᴀ ᵹſᴀıneᴀṁlᴀ ıᴀꝺ, 'however hateful they be' (trans. 'be they never so foul').

(2) a here takes h before vowels. What is said of last under (A) applies here.

(3) 'Their' (ecl.): see remarks under (A). These forms, in union with ré, tré, fá, become ré na, tré na, fá na; not to be confounded with ré a, 'by which'; tré a, 'through which.'

a, *vocative particle.*

a, *rel. pr.* (ecl.), who, which.

(A) Never used in this sense in nom. or acc. Hence, 'the man who strikes,' an fear a ḃuaileas, is incorrect—1st, because a eclipses; 2nd, because it is never used in such constructions. The correct form is an fear ḃuaileas, or with D. by insertion of verbal prefix, an fear do ḃuaileas. Used extensively with preps., v.g. 'about whom I spoke,' air ar laḃair mé; 'in which is given,' ann a d-tugṫar.

Never takes after it the relative tense which is intended to supply the absence of a relative pronoun in the nom. and acc. cases.

(B) That which, what; Lat., 'id quod,' 'ea quae,' in nom. and acc. case. *Dem. rel. pr.* Never takes relative tense, but is followed by the indirect forms of verbs: 'what you have,' 'ea quae habes,' a b-fuil agad. In union with preps. it takes the forms, aga, air a, ann a, da, &c.

ab, *see* atáim.

a b-fad uaḋ, far from it, on the contrary.

absdal, *m.*, Apostle; -ail, *g. s.*

absolóid, *f.*, absolution; -e, *g. s.*

aċ, *for* aċt.

a ċéile, his fellow, one another.

acfuinn, *f.*, power; -e, *g. s.*

aċt, but.

aḋḃar, *m.*, cause; -air, *g. s.*

adeirim, I say; deir, *3rd s. pres.*; dubairt, *3rd sg. perf.*; ráḋ, *inf.*; déarṫa, *pass. part.*; mar ——, so to speak.

adṁáil, *inf.*, confess.

adṁálaċ, *m.*, confession; -aiġ, *g. s.*; adṁálaċ, *g. p.*

aḋnáireaċ, modest.

ag, *prep.*, at, with; ag sin (lit. 'at that'), 'thus far' (what precedes in a context). ag so (lit. 'at this'), 'thus' (referring to what follows); here ag used extensively to express the possessor in the phrase, 'what thou hast,' &c., a b-fuil agud, &c., the Mid. Ir. verb, techtaim, 'I possess,' having fallen out of use.

aġaiḋ, *f.*, face; aiġṫe, *g. s.*; re h-aġaiḋ, for the benefit of; na h-aġaiḋ, against her.

agus, *cop. conj.*, and; Mid. Ir., 'ocus,' to which its pronunciation even now assimilates;—(2) *rel. conj.*, as; its correlatives being ionnan, coṁ, coṁ —— sin, &c.: cf. Latin, 'atque,' idem —— atque, aeque —— atque.

aibġidil, *f.*, alphabet; -e, *g. s.*

aiḃistin, *indecl.*, Augustine.

ᴀɪᴠ̇ʀɪosᴦ, brittle.

ᴀɪᴦɴeᴀᴠ̇, *m.*, mind; -ɴɪᴠ̇, *g. s.*

ᴀ́ɪʟʟ, *f.*, pleasure; -ʟʟe, *g. s.*

ᴀ́ʟuɪɴ, beautiful; ᴀ́ɪʟɴe, *comp.*

ᴀɪᴍ̇ᴠ̇eoɪɴ, *f.*, unwillingness; ᴠ̇'ᴀɪᴍ̇ᴠ̇eoɪɴ, notwithstanding.

ᴀɪᴍ̇ʟeᴀs, *m.*, harm; -ʟɪᴦ, *g. s.*

ᴀɪᴍ̇sɪᴦɪᴍ, I strike at; -eᴀᴦ, *pres. rel.*

ᴀɪᴍsɪʀ, *f.*, time; -e, *g. s.*

ᴀɪɴᴠ̇fɪos, *m.*, ignorance; -ɪᴦ, *g. s.*

ᴀɪɴᴠ̇íoᴦᴀʟᴛᴀċ, vindictive.

ᴀɪɴeóʟᴀċ, ignorant.

ᴀɪɴɪᴍ, *m.*, name (generally ᴀɪɴᴍ elsewhere); ᴀɴᴍᴀ, *g. s.*; ᴀɴᴍᴀɴɴᴀ, *n. p.*

ᴀɪɴᴍ̇ɪᴀɴ, *m.* and *f.*; -ᴀ and -ᴍ̇eɪɴe, *g. s.*

ᴀɪɴɴeɪs, *f.*, misery; -e, *g. s.*

ᴀɪɴɴeɪseᴀċ, miserable.

ᴀɪʀ, correct form ᴀᴦ, *prep.*, upon; often written *er* in Mid. Ir., and thus pronounced to this day both in Munster and Connaught. ɪᴀᴦ is often written similarly here, but is easily distinguished by the fact that ᴀɪᴦ aspirates, and ɪᴀᴦ eclipses. Used frequently to constitute adverbs, and conjs., and comp. preps. ᴀɪᴦ, on him; oᴦᴛᴀ, on them; ᴀɪᴦ bɪċ, at all; ᴀɪᴦ ċoᴦ, so that; ᴀɪᴦ ᴦeᴀᴠ̇, throughout; ᴀɪᴦ ᴦoɴ, for the sake.

ᴀ́ɪʀᴠ̇ (óᴦ), openly.

ᴀɪʀe, *f.*, watchfulness; —, *g. s.*

ᴀɪʀɪᴦ, special; *also* -e.

ᴀɪʀ soɴ, *prep.*, for the sake; gov. gen.

ᴀɪsɪoc, *m.*, restitution; -ᴦᴦ, *g. s.*

ᴀ́ɪᴛ, *f.*, place; -e, *g. s.*

ᴀɪᴛᴠ̇eoᴠ̇uɪᴦɪᴍ, I revive (in active sense); -uᴦᴀᴠ̇, *inf.*

ᴀɪᴛᴦɪoʀʀᴀ, *f.*, abridgment; —, *g. s.*

ᴀɪᴛɴɪᴦɪᴍ, I command; ᴀɪċɪɴ, *3rd s. perf.*; ᴀɪᴛɴɪᴦeᴀᴦ, *pres. pass.*; takes ᴠe of person who is commanded; *acc.*, of thing commanded.

ᴀɪᴛʀɪᴦe, *f.*, penance; —, *g. s.*

ᴀɪᴛʀɪᴦeᴀċ, penitent.

ᴀʟʟóᴠ̇ (ᴀ ɴ-), formerly.

ᴀᴍ, *m.*, time; ᴀᴍᴀ, *g. s.*

ᴀᴍᴀċ, out, forth.

ᴀᴍᴀ́ɪɴ, only.

ᴀᴍ̇ᴀʀc, *m.*, sight; -ᴀɪᴦc, *g. s.*

ᴀᴍ̇uɪʟ, as.

ᴀɴ, *def. art.*, the (Mid. Ir. *in*).

> (A) ᴀɴ in all singular cases, except *gen. sing. fem.*, which is ɴᴀ. In all plural cases ɴᴀ; with eclp. in *g. p.* The art. was originally ᴦᴀɴ; and when in union with many preps., the ᴦ reappears, v. g. ᴦɪᴦ ᴀɴ, ᴀɴɴ ᴦɴᴀ.

(B) Used to convert *adj.* into *subst.* :—

Cᴀꞇoꞁꞁꞇcᴄ,	.	Catholic.
nᴀ Cᴀꞇoꞁꞁꞇꞇꞁꞡe,	.	Catholics.

(C) An integral part of the *dem. pronom. adj.*, this, that, v.g. :—

ᴀn ṁꞁoᴄꞁú ꞃo, . this ill fame.

Note that the French and Irish often divide a term grammatically which is logically indivisible :—

This man, . . Cet homme-ci.

The word that the term qualifies or that qualifies the term is inserted between the divided parts. So in Irish :—

This man, . . ᴀn ꞃeᴀꞃ ꞃo.

(*See* ꞃꞁn, ꞃo.)

(D), used often to form compound adverbs and preps. :—

ᴀn ꞃeᴀ́ꞓ,	.	. during.
ᴀn ꞇᴀn,	.	. when, &c.

ᴀnᴀcꞃᴀᴄ, painful.

ᴀnᴀṁ, *m.*, soul (*f.* in old Ir.); ᴀnṁᴀ, *g. s.*; ᴀnmᴀnnᴀ, *n. p.*; ᴀnmᴀnn, *g. p.*

ᴀnᴀpᴀꞁᴓ, untimely.

ᴀncᴀ́ꞁneᴀ́ꞓ, *m.*, blasphemy.

ᴀncúṁᴀᴄꞇᴀᴄ, violent; -ᴀ, *pl.*

ᴀnṁóꞃᴀ́n, *m.*, very many; ᴀ́ꞁn, *g. s.*

ᴀnn, in.

ᴀnn ꞅꞁn, then, there.

ᴀnꞇoꞁꞁ, *f.*, depraved will; -oꞁᴀ, *g. s.*

ᴀoꞓᴀꞁꞃe, *m.*, shepherd; —, *g. s.*

ᴀoꞁnꞁeᴀꞇ, *f.*, one-half; -ꞁeꞁꞇe, *g. s.*

ᴀoꞁnneᴀᴄ, anyone.

ᴀoꞁnꞃeᴀᴄᴀ́ꞓ, *m.*, one sin; -ꞁᴓ, *g. s.*

ᴀoꞁnꞇeᴀꞡᴀꞅꞡ, *m.*, one catechism; -ᴀꞁꞃꞡ, *g. s.*

ᴀoꞁnꞇeᴀnꞡᴀ, *f.*, one tongue; -ꞡᴀꞁꞓ, *d. s.*

ᴀoꞁꞅ, *f.*, age; -e, *g. s.*

ᴀon, one (asp.).

ᴀonᴀꞓꞓᴀꞃ, *m.*, one cause; ᴀꞁꞃ, *g. s.*

ᴀoncoꞃ, *m.*, any way; -ᴄuꞁꞃ, *g. s.*

ᴀonꞡnoꞇuꞁꞡe, *f.*, one affair (with others *m.*); —, *g. s.*

ᴀonoꞁc, *m.*, one evil; -uꞁꞁc, *g. s.*

ᴀonꞡꞡᴀ́ꞁꞁe, *f.*, any shadow; —, *g. s.*

ᴀoncoꞃᴀ́ꞓ, *m.*, one fruit; -ᴀꞁꞓ, *g. s.*; ꞇoꞃᴄᴀ, *n. p.*

ᴀonꞇuꞁꞡꞁm, I consent; -ꞇuꞡᴀꞓ, *inf.*

ᴀoꞅ, *m.*, folk; ᴀoꞁꞃ, *g. s.*

ᴀoѕóᵹ, *m.*, the young; -óɪᵹ, *g. s.*

ᴀ́ʀ, *poss. pronom. adj.*, our (ecl.); nᴀʀ n-ᴏɪᴀɪᴅ, lit. (in our sequel) in the sequel; Mid. Ir., i n-ar ndiaid (*Pass. and Hom.* 60).

ᴀʀ, *impers. verb*, says.

ᴀʀ, *for* ɪᴀʀ; ᴀʀ nᴏɪᴀɪᴅ, in the sequel.

ᴀʀ, in form nᴀċ ᴀʀ = nᴀċᴀʀ; the form which ʀo takes when combined with nᴀċ; see nᴀċ; not to be confounded with following.

ᴀʀ, in form ᴀnn ᴀʀ cóɪʀ, 'in which it is right,' ᴀг ᴀʀ ḃʀéɪᴏɪʀ. Here the ᴀ in ᴀʀ is *rel. pr.*, its eclipsing nasal being absorbed by ʀ. ᴀnn ᴀ n-ʀo. For the meaning of ʀ in this form see ᴀᴄᴀɪm.

ᴀ́ʀᴏꜰʟᴀɪᴄ, *m.*, chief lord; —, *g. s.*

ᴀ́ʀᴏѕᴀᵹᴀʀᴄ, *m.*, high priest; -ᴀɪʀᴄ, *g. s.*

ᴀ́ʀᴏυɪᵹɪm, I raise; -ᴏυᵹᴀᴅ, *inf.*

ᴀ́ʀѕυɪᴅ, old; -ʀυɪᵹe, *pl.*

ᴀѕ, from.

ᴀѕᴏɪᵹ, within (literally 'in the house').

ᴀѕᴄeᴀċ, into the house, within.

ᴀᴄᴀɪm (Lat. asto), I exist, I am; called the substantive verb; found here chiefly in the following forms:—

Simple Forms :—

ᴄᴀ, ᴀᴄᴀ́, *3rd s. pres.*; ᴀᴄᴀɪᴏ, *3rd pl. pres.*; bíᴅ, *3rd pl. cons. pres.*; bɪᴀɪᴅ, *3rd s. fut.*; bɪᴀᴅ, *3rd s. cond.*; beɪᴏíʀ, *3rd pl. cond.*; beɪċ, *inf.*

Relative Forms :—

ᴄᴀ, ᴀᴄᴀ́; bíoʀ, *cons. pres rel.*; bɪᴀʀ, *fut. rel.*

Enclitic Forms :—

(*i. e.* after ᵹo, ní, nᴀċ, preps., with rel., &c.) b-ꜰυɪl, *3rd s. pres.*; b-ꜰυɪlɪᴏ, *3rd pl. pres.*; ʀᴀbᴀɪᴏ, *3rd pl. pres. subj.*

IS (*called the Assertive Verb.*)

Simple Forms :—

ɪʀ, *pres.*; b, for buᴅ, *cond.*

Relative Forms :—

ɪʀ, *pres.*; buʀ, *fut.*

Enclitic Forms :—

Present.

ní (is not); munᴀ (unless is); cʀeuᴅ (what is); ᵹɪᴅ bé (whoever he be); ᵹuʀ, ᵹuʀ ᴀb (that is); nᴀċ (is not), *interrog.*; ᴅᴀ́ʀ (of whom are); ᴅᴀ́ʀ (to whom is); nᴀċ (that is not); cʀé ᴀʀ ꜰéɪᴏɪʀ (through which is possible); le ᴀʀ ᴀb (to whom are); nᴀċ (who are not).

Past.

ᴀᴦ ᴀɴ ᴅꝼéɪᴏɪᴩ (from which was possible); nᴀċ ᴀɴ ᴅꝼéɪᴏɪᴩ (whioh was not possible), *or* that (*conj.*) was not possible.

Conditional.

(Enclitic), ᴦᴏ mᴀᴅ, may (it) be.

The distinction between ɪᴦ and ᴀᴄáɪm cannot be scientifically understood until an agreement is come to as to the precise meaning of 'is' in the simple question, 'Peter is a lawyer'; in other words, an agreement as to the meaning of the copula in affirmative propositions. The signification of the 'copula' is a question that goes down to the very roots of metaphysics and logic; and the question as to its meaning will be solved differently and in a contradictory sense by the followers, respectively, of Mill, Hamilton, Kant, and Aristotle.

Students of Aristotelian and of scholastic philosophy will recognize that ɪᴦ affirms "in recto" the objective identity of two ideas: ɪᴦ mɪᴦe ᴦᴏʟuᴦ ᴀn ᴏᴏṁᴀɪn, 'I am the light of the world.' The object denoted by the term 'I' and the object denoted by the term 'light of the world' are one and the same thing.

Again, in propositions, the subject is the matter, the attribute is the form. It is true to say that the form "in facto esse" contains the matter, and that consequently the matter is in it. The Irish way of saying 'Peter is a priest' illustrates this truth: ᴄᴀ ᴩeᴀᴏᴀᴩ nᴀ ꝼᴀᴦᴀᴩᴄ, 'Peter is in his priest.' The person represented by the term 'Peter'—i. e. the matter—is contained in the form 'priest.' This form 'priest,' however, is itself a universal—that is, capable of being predicated of John, and Peter, and James. It is clear that this form 'priest,' as individualized in Peter, is not identical with the form 'priest' found in John and James. To bring out this fact we may say then, with the Irish, 'Peter is in *his* priest.' Of course, as in all affirmative propositions, we have here affirmed the objective identity of two ideas. This, however, is affirmed only in "in obliquo"; and it is stated "in recto" that the *matter* 'Peter' is contained in the *form* 'priest.' Hence, as the grammarians say, if we want to describe the condition, quality, and state of the subject, we use ᴀᴄáɪm; if we want to say that two notions represent the same object, we use ɪᴦ.

ᴀᴄᴀɪʀ, *m.*, father; ᴀᴄᴀᴩ, *g. s.*; ᴀɪċᴩeᴀᴄᴀ, *n. p.*; ᴀɪċᴩeᴀᴄ, *g. p.*

ᴀᴄċuɪnᴦe, *f.*, petition; —, *g. s.*

ᴀᴄċumuɪʀ, brief; -e, *pl.*

ᴀᴄnuᴀᴏuɪᴣɪm, I renew; ᴀᴄnuᴀᴏuᴦᴀᴏ, *inf.*

ᴀᴄʀuɪᴣɪm, I change; -ᴩuᴦᴀᴏ, *inf.*

ᴀᴄᴦmuᴀɪnɪm, I think again; -neᴀᴏ, *inf.*

ᴀᴄᴦuɪᴏɪm, I re-establish; ᴀᴄꝼuɪᴏɪuᴣeᴀᴏ, *inf.*

ᴀᴄċuɪᴄɪm, *f.*, relapse; -e, *g. s.*

bᴀɪnne, *m.*, milk; —, *g. s.*

báɪʀʀeuᴏᴄʀom, light-headed.

baisdeaḋ, *m.*, baptism.

baisdim, I baptize; bairoeaḋ, *inf.*

'baoġlaċ, dangerous; -uiġe, *comp.*

baos, *m.*, vanity; baoir, *g. s.*

bárrġlór, *m.*, boasting; -óir, *g. s.*

bás, *m.*, death; báir, *g. s.*

basġaim, I destroy; barġaḋ, *inf.*; -ġaiṁċe, *g. s.*

beaċt, exact.

beaġ, little; biġ, *g. s.*, *m.*; beaġa, *pl.*; ġo naċ beaġ, that it is enough.

beaġán, *m.*, few; -áin, *g. s.*

beaġnaċ, almost.

bealaċ, *m.*, road; bealaiġ, *g. s.*

beanaim, I extract (when followed by ar); when followed by ré, I belong to; buain, *inf.*, reaping; beanar, *pres. rel.*

beann, *f.*, regard; -nna, *g. s.*

béarla, *m.*, English; —, *g. s.*

beaṫa, *f.*, life; —, *g. s.*

beaṫuiġim, I feed; -uġaḋ, *inf.*; -ċuiġear, *pres. pass.*

beir, *see* dobeirim.

beirim, I bear; breiṫ, *inf.*; -ruġaḋ, *perf. pass.*, was born.

beoḋuġim, I animate; -uġaḋ, *inf.*

béul, *m.*, mouth; béil, beóil, *g. s.*

beus, *m.*, manner; beura, *g. s.*; —, *n. p.*; béar, *g. p.*; beuraiḃ, *d. p.*

bḟéidir, perhaps (buḋ féidir).

bḟéidir, *see* aċáim.

biaḋ, *m.*, food; biḋ, *g. s.*

bíoḋ, although.

biṫ, *m.*, world; beaṫa, *g. s.*; air biṫ, (any) in the world.

blas, *m.*, taste; blair, *g. s.*

blaisim, I taste; blaraḋ, *inf.*; blairodar, *3rd pl. perf.*

bláṫ, *m.*, flower; -ċa, *g. s.*

bliaḋain, *f.*, year; -ḋna, *g. s.*

boċt, poor; boiċte, *g. s.*, *f.*

borraḋ, *m.*, budding; -aiḋ, *g. s.*

bráṫaċ, eternal.

bráṫair, *m.*, brother (in an order); braṫar, *g. s.*

breaṫaitriġe, *f.*, penance imposed by priest; —, *g. s.*

breiteaṁ, *m.*, judge; breiċiṁ, breiteaṁan, *g. s.*

breiteaṁnas, *m.*, judgment; sentence; -uir, *g. s.*

breuġaċ, lying.

briaṫar, *f.*, word; bréiṫre, *g. s.*; bréiṫir, *d. s.*

briġ, *f.*, force; -ġe, *g. s.*

bríoṫṁaṅ, strong.

bṙisim, I break; bṙiṡeaḋ, *inf.*

bṙosouiġim, I excite; -uġaḋ, *inf.*

bṙúiġneaċ, quarrelsome.

buaiḋ, *f.*, victory; -aiḋe, *g. s.*

buain, *see* beanaim.

buille, *m.*, blow; —, *g. s.*; -aiṙ aġaiḋ, stroke in advance, so much done.

bun, *m.*, foundation; buin, *g. s.*

bunúḋas, *m.*, matter; -aiṙ, *g. s.*

bunúḋasaċ, fundamental, chief.

cáċ, everyone; cáiċ, *g. s.*

cailleaṁuin, *f.*, loss; -ṁna, *g. s.*

caillim, I lose; cailleaḋ, *inf.*

cáin, *f.*, tax, penalty; -e, cánaċ, *g. s.*

cáinim, I revile; -eaḋ, *inf.*

caitim, I spend; -eaḋ, *inf.*

cáirḋe, *f.*, delay, respite.

calcaim, I harden; -aḋ, *inf.*

caonḋúċract, *f.*, devotion; -a, *g. s.*

carnaim, I heap up; -aḋ, *inf.*

catoilice, Catholic; -ciġe, *n. p.*

ceaċtaṙ, either.

ceaḋ, *m.*, permission; -ḋa, *g. s.*

céaḋna, same; maṙ an gcéaḋna, likewise.

cealg, *f.*, deceit; ceilge, *g. s.*

cealgaċ, deceitful.

ceana, already.

ceangailim, I bind; ceangal, *inf.*

ceann, *m.*, head; cinn, *g. s.*

ceannuiġim, I purchase; ceannaċ, *inf.*

ceapaim, I form, I design; ceapaḋ, *inf.*

ceart, right.

ceasḋ, *f.*, question; -a, *g. s.*

céilliġe, prudent.

ceirtḃreiteaṁnas, *m.*, just judgment; -uiṙ, *g. s.*

céuḋ, first (wrongly aspirated in some grammars).

céuḋ, a hundred.

céuḋraḋ, *m.*, sense, opinion; -a, *g. s.*

céusaim, I torment; céaṡaḋ, *inf.*, which as noun denotes the ' passion.'

ciall, *f.*, sense; céille, *g. s.*

ciallluiġim, I signify; -uġaḋ, *inf.*

cípú, *see* oócim.

cineaú, *m.*, race ; -ıú, *g. s.* ; cınıúeaca, *pl.*, the Gentiles.

cion, *f.*, sin ; cıonaú, *g. s.* ; cıonca, *n. p.*

cionpac, *m.*, cause, occasion ; -a, *g. s.*

cionn, *m.*, head ; or a cíonn pın, moreover.

cionnas, how (*ci indus*, what manner).

cioncac, guilty ; -pé, responsible for.

cioncuızim, I sin ; -uᵹaú, *inf.*

cláirín, *m.*, hornbook.

clann, *f.*, children ; cloınne, *g. s.*

claoclo(ú), *m.*, change ; -oıú, *g. s.*

claon, inclined.

claonaú, *m.*, inclination ; claonca, *g. s.*

cleaccaim, I use ; I am wont, accustomed; -aú, *inf.*

cloc, *f.*, stone ; cloıce, *g. s.*

clóú, *m.*, print ; -a, *g. s.*

clóúaúóir, *m.*, printer ; -óra, *g. s.*

cluinim, I hear ; cloy, *inf.* ; cloınpıo, *3rd pl. fut.*

cneasoa, honest.

cnis, *f.*, warp (in a loom) ; -e, *g. s.* ; namaú cnıpe, bosom enemy.

coᵹuas, *m.*, conscience ; -uaıy, *g. s.*

coıúce, ever.

coiṁceanᵹal, *m.*, conspiracy.

coiṁúe, *m.* (Mid. Ir. *coimdiu*), Lord ; —, *g. s.*

coiṁoıomúuıúeac, so ungrateful.

coiṁéaúaim, I keep, preserve ; coiṁéuo, *inf.*

coiṁfreaᵹraim, I correspond ; -ᵹra, *inf.*

coiṁıúceac, foreign ; -a, *pl.*

coiṁlíonaim, I fulfil ; -aú, *inf.*

coiṁminic, as often (as).

coiṁneaṁᵹrónac, as spotless.

coiṁcionólaim, I assemble ; -cıonól, *inf.*

coinᵹioll, *m.*, condition ; -ᵹıll, *g. s.*

coir, *f.*, sin ; -e, *g. s.*

cóir, *adj.*, right ; córa, *comp.*

coirlicin, *f.*, odd letter ; -lıcpeaca, *n. p.*

coirceac, guilty.

coiccionn, general ; -cınne, *comp.*

colann, *f.*, body ; colla, colna, *g. s.*

coṁ, *corr. adv.*, so, as. Does not occur here except in comp. with adjectives and adverbs. Its relative *conj.* is aᵹuy : coiṁminic aᵹuy ṁeapuıo, 'as often as they think.'

coṁaιnle, f., counsel, council ; —, g. s.
coṁampláċ, as greedy.
coṁaʀsá, f., neighbour ; -aη, g. s.
coṁaʀċá, m., sign ; —, g. s.
coṁoáηa, so bold.
coṁooṁaιη, so deep.
coṁṗaoa, as long.
coṁṗoċaL, m., synonym ; -aιL, g. s.
coṁ§Laη, as pure.
coṁLuaċ, as soon.
coṁηuι§ιm, I dwell ; -§e, inf.
coṁʀac, m., combat.
coṁʀáṫ, m., discourse ; -áιṫ.
coṁʀoιnn, f., participation ; -onna, g. s.
coṁċʀom, just, even.
con§ṫaιm, I keep ; con§ṁaιL, inf.
con§naιm, I help ; con§naṁ, inf. ; -§anċa, g. s.
connʀáṫ, m., agreement ; connaṗċa, g. s.
conċus, m., account ; -uιʀ, g. s.
coʀ, m., case ; cuιʀ, g. s.
coʀʀṗocaL, m., odd word ; -aιL, g. s.
cosaṁLaċċ, f., probability ; -a, g. s.
cos§aιm, I hinder ; coʀ§, inf.
cosuιnιm, I cost ; coʀnaṁ, inf.
cʀáιṫċeaċ, pious.
cʀaos, m., gluttony ; cʀaoιʀ, g. s.
cʀé, f., creed.
cʀeapaLċa, entangled.
cʀeιoιm, I believe ; cʀeιoeaṫ, cʀeιoeaṁuιn, inf.
cʀeuo, what ?
cʀíoso, Christ.
cʀíosoaṁuιL, Christlike, Christian.
cʀíosouι§e, Christian.
cʀιoċnuι§ιm, I tremble ; -u§aṫ, inf.
cʀoιṫe, m., heart ; —, g. s.
cʀuaṫṁuιnéaLaċ, pl., stiff-necked ; -a, pl.
cʀuaιṫ, hard.
cʀuιnnι§ιm, I collect ; -ιu§aṫ, inf.
cʀuċ, m., condition, state ; cʀoċa, g. s.
cʀuċuι§ιm, I create, prove ; -ċu§aṫ, inf.
cʀuċuι§ċeóιʀ, m., Creator ; -óʀa, g. s.
cuaιṫ, see ċéιṫιm.

cuⁱbe, suitable.

cuⁱꝺ, *f.*, part ; conċᴀ, conᴀ, *g. s.*

cuⁱꝺⁱɠⁱm, I help ; -ⁱuɢᴀꝺ, *inf.*

cuⁱnɢ, *f.*, yoke ; -e, *g. s.*

cuⁱnⁱm, I put; cuꞃ, *inf.* ; cuꞃ ᴀ n-ɢníoṁ, to put in practice ; -ᴀ leⁱċ nᴀ h-eᴀɢ-luⁱꞃe, to accuse the Church ; cuꞃ ꝺ'ꝼⁱᴀċᴀⁱb ᴀⁱꞃ, to put an obligation on ; —— ꞃompᴀ, to propose to themselves, resolve ; cuⁱꞃeᴀnn, *cons. pres.*

ċum, *see* ꝺoċum.

cuṁᴀċcᴀ, *m.*, power ; —, *g. s.*

cumᴀⁱm, I form ; -ᴀꝺ, *inf.*

cumᴀoⁱn, *f.*, communion ; -e, *g. s.*

cumᴀɢ, *m.*, power ; -ᴀⁱꞃ, *g. s.*

cúṁꝺuⁱɠceóⁱꞃ, *m.*, protector ; -óꞃᴀ, *g. s.*

ꝺᴀ́, to his, &c. ; *see* ꝺo.

ꝺᴀ́, of which ; *see* ꝺe, ꝺᴀ, and ᴀ.

ꝺᴀ́ (*asp.*), two.

ꝺᴀ́ (*ecl.*), if.

ꝺᴀⁱlle, *f.*, blindness ; —, *g. s.*

ꝺᴀⁱnɢeᴀn, *m.*, stronghold ; -ɢⁱn, *g. s.*

ꝺᴀllᴀⁱm, I blind ; -ᴀꝺ, *inf.*

ꝺᴀllꞃᴀꝺᴀꞃc, *m.*, blindness ; -ᴀⁱꞃc.

ꝺᴀ́n, *m.*, verse ; ꝺᴀⁱn, ꝺᴀ́nᴀ, *g. s.*

ꝺᴀoⁱceᴀṁuⁱl, base.

ꝺᴀonnᴀ, human.

ꝺᴀoꞃsmᴀċc, *m.-f.*, bondage ; -ᴀ, *g. s.*

ꝺᴀꞃ, *for* ꝺe ᴀ (rel.) ꞃo, followed by past tense.

ꝺᴀꞃ, ꝺ'ᴀꞃ, of whom are, to whom is : see ᴀcᴀ́ⁱm.

ꝺ'ᴀꞃ, *for* ꝺe ᴀꞃ, of our.

ꝺᴀꞃᴀ, second.

ꝺᴀ́ ꞃíꞃⁱꝺ, really.

ꝺᴀ́sᴀċcᴀċ, fierce ; -ᴀⁱɠ, *d. s.*, *f.*

ꝺe, from, out of. Not appearing here as a separate prep. as in comp. with the article and before nouns, it takes the same form as ꝺo. Easily recognized in pronom. compounds—

ꝺe, from him ; ꝺⁱ, from her ; ꝺíob, from them.

Used much in partitive sense—cuⁱꝺ ꝺíob, a part of them, &c.

ꝺeᴀɠꝺuⁱne, *m.*, good man ; —, *g. s.*

ꝺeᴀɠoⁱꝺe, *m.*, good instructor ; —, *g. s.*

ꝺeᴀɠoⁱꝺeᴀs, *m.*, good instruction ; -ꝺⁱꞃ, *g. s.*

ꝺeᴀlbᴀⁱm, I compose ; -ᴀꝺ, *inf.*

ⱱeⱺⱤⱦⱥ, certain.

ⱱeⱥⱤⱨⱥⱱ, *m.*, forgetfulness; -ⱥⱽ, *g. s.*

ⱱéⱥⱤⱨⱥⱳ, *see* ⱱoním.

ⱱeⱦⱨín, certain.

ⱱeⱳⱤ, *see* ⱥⱱeⱳⱤⱨ.

ⱱéⱳⱤꞇ, *f.*, alms; -e, *g. s.*

ⱱeⱳⱤeⱥⱳ, *m.*, end; -ⱳⱽ, *g. s.*

ⱱeóⱦ, *f.*, end; ꝼⱥ-, in fine.

ⱱeóⱳn, *f.*, will; ⱱo ——, willingly.

ⱱeónuⱳⱦⱳm, I vouchsafe; -ⱦeⱥⱽ, *inf.*

ⱱeóⱤ, *m.*, tear; -óⱳⱤ, -óⱤⱥ, *g. s.*

ⱱéunⱥⱳ, *see* ⱱoním.

ⱱⱳⱥ, *m.*, God; ⱱé, *g. s.*

ⱱⱳⱥⱽⱥⱡ, *m.*, devil; -uⱳⱡ, *g. s.*

ⱱⱳⱥⱳⱽ, *f.*, nⱥ ——, after her.

ⱱíⱡeⱥⱤꞇⱥ, banished.

ⱱíⱡeⱥⱦⱥⱳm, I digest; -ⱡeⱥⱦⱥⱽ, *inf.*

ⱱíoⱠoⱳⱦⱦⱳꞇe, implacable.

ⱱíoⱦⱥⱳⱡⱳm, I avenge; -ⱡꞇ, *inf.*

ⱱíoⱦⱥⱡꞇⱥⱤ, *m.*, vengeance; -uⱳⱤ, *g. s.*

ⱱíoⱦⱽⱥⱳⱡ, *f.*, loss, want; -ⱥⱡⱥ, *g. s.*

ⱱíoⱦⱤⱥⱳⱤeⱥⱠ, zealous.

ⱱíoⱡumⱥ, correctly ⱱíoⱦⱡumⱥ, *g. s.* of ⱱíoⱦⱡuⱳm, act of gleaning, compiling.

ⱱⱳomⱽuⱳⱱeⱥⱠ, ungrateful.

ⱱíoⱦⱳoⱡⱥⱳm, I censure; -ⱥⱽ, *inf.*

ⱱⱳonⱦⱳⱳⱡꞇⱥ, firm.

ⱱⱳoⱤⱤuⱳⱤꞇe, rash.

ⱱíⱤⱳⱦⱳm, I direct; -ⱳuⱦⱥⱽ, *inf.*

ⱱíⱤⱡⱳⱦⱳm, I relinquish, put aside, -ⱳuⱦⱥⱽ, *inf*

ⱱíꞇⱠeⱥnnⱥⱳ, *m.*, destruction.

ⱱíꞇⱠeⱥnnuⱳⱦⱳm, I behead, destroy; -uⱦⱥⱽ, *inf.*

ⱱíꞇⱠéⱳⱡⱡⱳⱦ, foolish.

ⱱíꞇⱠⱳoⱡⱡ, *m.*, diligence; -Ⱡⱳⱡⱡ, *g. s.*

ⱱíꞇⱠⱤeⱳⱱⱳⱨeⱥⱠ, unbelieving.

ⱱⱳúⱡꞇⱥⱳm, I renounce; -ⱥⱽ, *inf.*

ⱱⱡⱳⱦeⱥⱳ, *m.*, law; -ⱦⱳⱽ, *g. s.*

ⱱⱡⱳⱦⱳm, *m.*, I owe; -ⱦeⱥⱽ, *inf.*

ⱱⱡⱳⱱoⱳonⱥⱠ, lawful.

ⱱo, prefix, before past tenses.

ⱱo, thy (*asp.*).

ⱱo, *prep.*, to, &c.: ⱱó, to him; ⱱóⱳⱽ, to them; ⱱúⱳnn, to us. These forms are always aspirated after vowels, aspirated consonants, and Ɱ. In other cases

there is some variance in the usage. In constant use before the infinitive, and forming, with the infinitive, what may be called a gerund, *i. e.* part of speech fulfilling the functions of verb, noun, and even of adjective, v. g. ᴅo buaLaᵭ. This form, O'Donovan, with others, calls the infinitive, which it certainly is not, and its grammatical laws are altogether different from those of infinitive. Its several rules are these :—when the verb is transitive the object of the verb must be expressed ; when the verb is intransitive the subject of the verb must be expressed. Thus—

> ' It is right to love God,' ιꞃ cóιꞃ ᴅιa ᴅo ᵹꞃaᵭuᵹaᵭ.

In this last instance we have the gerund discharging its functions of noun and verb—noun, because it is nom. case to ιꞃ ; verb, because it governs ᴅιa.   It corresponds here to the Latin infin. (itself a gerundial form).

> Justum est amare Deum.

O'Donovan's rule on this subject (p. 387) is not only inadequate, but incorrect ; but his examples are valuable—

(1) ᴅubaιꞃc ꞃé Lιom ᴅuL ᵹo Coꞃcaιᵹ. 'he told me to go to Cork.'
In this phrase he says that the rule is, when the governed verb is one expressing motion or gesture, the sign ᴅo is never expressed.   He lays claim to be the first discoverer of this rule.   How untenable this rule is appears from page 363 of the *Grammar*, where he gives the following examples :—

(2) aᵹ caιꞃnᵹιꞃe Pácꞃaιc ᴅo ᴄeaᴄc ann, ' predicting that Patrick would come thither.'

(3) ιaꞃ ᵹ-cLoꞃ ᴅι an cꞃannᴄuꞃ ᴅo ᴄuιcιm aꞃ a mac, ' when she heard the lot fell upon her Son.'

Surely, ᴄeaᴄc and ᴄuιcιm are both verbs of motion or gesture ; and if the rule were correct, ᴅo should not be found before these infinitives.

The true explanation of those forms is : In No. 1 no subject is expressed, and the infinitive is not required to assume the governing or agreeing function of a verb.   In No. 2 and No. 3 the subject of the intransitive verbs is expressed, and therefore recourse must be had to the gerund forms ᴅo ᴄeaᴄc, ᴅo ᴄuιcιm.

Again, we have here, sect. 1—

> ' Several things intended . . . to move the will, practise virtue, and to fly vice.'

> . . . ᴄum na ꞃubáιLce ᴅo ᵹnáιᴄ-ᴄLeaᴄcaᵭ aᵹuꞃ (2) an ᴅubaιLce ᴅo ꞃeaᴄnaᵭ.

The first construction O'Donovan fails to explain, and even goes so far as to say, " that it is not to be approved of."   Yet it is a most common form in the Middle and Modern Irish of the best authors.   It would be as reasonable to condemn a Latin writer for saying—

> ' Virtutis exercendae causa
> Vitiumque vitandi.'

The Irish gerund, vo bualuᵹ, though indeclinable, is capable of standing in nearly all relations of gender, number, and case.   Thus, in the phrase—

(a) Ir éiᵹin ceiṫre neiṫe vo veunaṁ, ' there are four things to be done.' Nom. sing. to verb ir governing neiṫe in the acc. pl.

(b) Ċum na ruḃailce vo ᵹnáiṫċleaċtaḃ. Gen. sing., governed by ċum, and attracting ruḃáilce, g. s. f.

(c) an vuḃáilce vo ḟeaċnaḃ. Gen. sing., governed by ċum, and governing vuḃáilce in the acc.

(d) . . . air foclaiḃ coiṁiṫⱦeaċa vo ḟeaċnaḃ, ' (endeavours were made) to avoid foreign expressions.'—(Sect. xiii., line 1.)

Dat. pl., with foclaiḃ, d. p. m.

Cf. Latin—

Dedi operam verbis alienigenis vitandis ;

and cf. Cicero—

Meum laborem hominum periculis sublevandis impertio.

These gerundial constructions are to be distinguished from a simple case where vo bualuᵹ, without preceding subject or object, is simply used to express a purpose ; thus, tainic ré vo ṫeaᵹarᵹ an poḃail, ' he came to teach the people.' Here the infinitive appears as a verbal noun in the dative case, governed by vo, and governing the objective genitive poḃail.

Besides the examples above given of the gerund, there is another form of phrase in which, with a transitive verb, we have subject and object expressed ; thus—

' This is the love of God, that we keep His commandments.'

(e) . . . rinne vo ċoiṁéuv a aiṫeantaḃ.

In this phrase we have the gerund agreeing with the subject rinne, and governing aiṫeantaḃ in the gen. In this construction the subject must always precede, and the object must follow the gerund.

Cf. here, sect. 36—

' Humbly beseeching God that his own unworthiness may not put a hindrance,' &c.

(f) . . . ᵹan a ainneir féin vo ċur toirmirᵹ.
ainneir, subject preceding gerund.
toirmirᵹ, object following gerund.

(See the fuller treatment in Pass.-Hom. Gloss., pp. 650, sqq., sub voce).

For those who desire to compare further Latin and Irish construction, it may be interesting to note that Donlevy, in examples b and c, breaks off from what may be called the gerundive participle, and betakes himself to the gerund proper. So does Cicero, speaking of M. Antony, ' The question is, whether power be given to M. Antony to oppress the republic to make a present of the lands,' &c.—

' Utrum facultas detur opprimendae reipublicae, agrorum condonandi.'

The infinitive in Latin is strong enough to act as a verb in nom. and acc. relation. The Irish infinitive, bualáð, has not this strength, but requires to be reinforced by the prep. ðo. The Latin infin. is not strong enough to act in oblique cases as a verb and noun. Hence the recourse to the gerund and gerundive participle. The Irish gerund, ðo bualáð, acts as—

> The Latin infinitive.
> ,,   gerund.
> ,,   gerundive participle.

The Latins do not use the prep. *sine*, without, with the gerundial forms; hence another term of phrase must be employed when a negative is to be used. The Irish gerund permits the use of the negative prep. ʒan (see above, example (*f*)).

ðobeiрim, I give; beiр, 3 *s. pres.*; cabaiрc, *inf.*; cuʒ, 3 *s. perf.*

ðoðрón, *m.*, sorrow; -óin, *g. s.*

ðocaр, *m.*, harm; -aiр, *g. s.*

ðocím, I see; ð'ḟeicрin, *inf.*; ðocíрð, 3rd *s. fut.*; ðocíceaр.

ðocoimsiʒce, incomprehensible.

ðocum, *prep.*, towards, *govs. gen.* Includes also, not only motion towards a term, but arrival at it—cáinic cum céille, &c. Written usually cum, with aspiration which denotes its original form. Used much here to express a purpose, with the gerund form ðo bualáð; *see* ðo.

ðoʒeiðim, I find, obtain; ḟaʒbáil, *inf.*; ʒeiðið, 3rd *s. pres.*; ʒéaðuið, 3rd pl. *fut.*; ḟuaiр, 3rd *s. perf.*

ðoilʒeas, *m.*, sorrow; -ʒiр, *g. s.*

ðoimeasða, inestimable.

ðomán, *m.*, world; -ain, *g. s.*

ðomuin, deep; ðoimne, *comp.*

ðomúince, ill-taught.

ðo(ʒ)ním, I do, make; ðéunað, *inf.*; -ca, *g. s.*; ní, 3rd *s. pres.*; níceaр, *pres. pass.*; ðéuna, 3rd *s. fut.*; ðéuрnað, *perf. pass.*; рinneað, *perf. pass.*

ðo рéiр, according to.

ðoрca, obscure.

ðoрcaðus, *m.*, darkness; -uiр, *g. s.*

ðosʒaoilce, indissoluble.

ðo caoð, regarding.

ðóccas, *m.*, hope; -aiр, *g. s.*

ðрeam, *m.*, people; -a, *g. s.*

ðрeas, partly.

ðрoðlásac, licentious; -aiʒ, *d. s. f.*

ðрocclaonað, *m.*, bad inclination; -nca, *g. s.*

ðрocnós, *m.*, bad habit; -óiр, *g. s.*

ðрocsompla, *m.*, bad example; —, *g. s.*

ðрoicðeusac, wicked.

droiċċleaċtaḋ, *m.*, bad practice; -aiḋ, *g. s.*
droiċiomċar, *m.*, bad conduct; -air, *g. s.*
droiċṁéineaċ, of bad desires.
droiċṁian, *m.* and *f.*, bad desire; -a, *g. s.*
drong, *f.*, people; droinge, *g. s.*
drúis, *f.*, impurity; -e, *g. s.*
drúiseaṁuil, lascivious.
dúal, *m.*, duty, -uail, *g. s.*
dualgas, *m.*, duty; -ais, *g. s.*
duḃáilce, *f.*, vice; —, *g. s*,
duḃainḃḟios, *m.*, utter (black) ignorance; -ḟis, *g. s.*
duḃairt, *see* adeirim.
duilleóg, *f.*, page; -eóige, *g. s.*
duine, *m.*, man; —, *g. s.*; daoine, *n. p.*; daoiniḃ, doiniḃ, *d. p.*
dúitċe, *f.*, estate; —, *g. s.*, dúitċiḋeaḋ, *g. p.*
dul, *see* téiḋim.
dútċas, *m.*, birth-place; -ais, *g. s.*
dútráċtaċ, earnest.

é, *see* sé.
eaḋón, that is (the equivalent of .i. in Mid. Irish). As the Greek ὅτι is often best translated in English by inverted commas, so the abbreviation .i. may be generally rendered literally (. . .)
eagar, *m.*, order; -air, *g. s.*
eagla, *f.*, fear; —, *g. s.*
eagluis, *f.*, church; -e, *g. s.*
eagna, *f.*, wisdom; —, *g. s.*
eaguil, *f.*, fear.
easbog, *m.*, bishop; -oig, *g. s.*
easḃuiḋ, *f.*, want; —, *g. s.*
easmolaim, I reproach; -aḋ, *inf.*
éigceart, unjust.
éigean, *m.*, necessity; -gin, *g. s.*
éigeas, *m.*, philosopher; -is, *g. s.*; -éigse, *n. p.*
éigin, some.
éire, *f.*, Ireland; -rionn, *g. s.*; -rinn, *d. s.*
éirġim, I rise; éirġe, *inf.*
éisdim, I listen; éisdeaċt, *inf.*
eól, *m.*, knowledge.
eólus, *m.*, knowledge; -uis, *g. s.*
eólgaċ, learned.
eóroip, *f.*, Europe.

éugaim, I die; éug, *inf.*

éugcórac, unjust: -aig, *comp.*

éugcosṁuil, unlike; -ṙaṁla, *pl.*

éugcruaiḃ, weak; -ige, *comp.*

éugsamuil, different; -ṁla, *pl.*

fá, *prep.*, under; written also fó, faoi. In Mid. Irish governs dat. and acc. Usually now governs dat., but here found with acc., fa cionta, with *art.* fa'n, *poss. pr.* 3rd *person;* fa na, with *rel.*, followed by ṅo, fa'ṅ and fa aṙ.

faḋa, long, far; faiḋe, *comp.*

fáġail, correctly faġḃáil; *see* ḋoġeiḃim.

fáġḃaim, I leave; -báil; -ġtaṙ, *pres. pass.*

fuil, *see* atáim.

fáiḃ, *m.*, prophet; —, *g. s.*

failliġe, *f.*, neglect; —, *g. s.*

faiṙim, I watch; faiṙe, *inf.*

fa leit, separately.

faoi lár, on the floor; ṙacaḃ —, should fall into neglect.

faoisiḋin, *f.*, confession; -e, *g. s.*

faṙaoṙ, alas!

fásaim, I grow; fáṙ, *inf.*

feact, *f.*, time.

fearġac, choleric.

feáṙṙ, better.

feas, *m.*, knowledge; -a, *g. s.*

feasac, known.

féiḋiṙ. In form it seems to correspond with Mid. Irish, fétaṙ, éciṙ, pass. forms of féaḋaim, 'I am able.' In modern use it has become a subst. or adj. not aspirated by D. after ní. Its general use is as indefinite predicate after iṙ, the subject being the infin. or gerund; *see* ḋo: iṙ féiḋiṙ ḋóiḃ an loġaḋ ḋo ġnóḃugaḋ, 'they can gain the indulgence.' (To gain the indulgence is *possible* for them, or *possibility* for them.) Written by K. éiḋiṙ, but pronounced as written by D. (O'Brien, *adj.*, Coney's *fem. subst.*)

féile, *f.*, liberality; —, *g. s.*

féin, *emph. particle*, self, very.

fiac, *m.*, debt; fiacaiḃ, *d. p.*; ... ata ḋ'fiacaiḃ oṙta ḋo cṙeiḋeaṁuin, '(things) which they are *obliged* to believe.'

fiaḋnuise, *f.*, presence; —, *g. s.*

fionnfaim, I see, I find; -aḋ, *inf.*

fíoṙ, true.

fíoṙaitṙeacus, *m.*, sincere repentance; -uiṙ, *g. s.*

fíoṙḋoilġíosac, sincerely sorry.

fíoṁaιċ, excellent.

fιοs, *m.*, knowledge; fιr, *g. s.*

fιοsruġaṁ, *m.*, question; -uιġċe, *g. s.*, *n. p.*

fírċearc, genuine justice.

fíre, true.

fíréanċaċc, *f.*, justice; -a, *g. s.*

fírιnne, *f.*, truth.

fírιnneaċ, true.

fιċċe, twenty; -ċιo, *pl.*

fιú, worthy.

flaιċιos, *m.*, kingdom; -ċιr, *g. s.*

focal, *m.*, word; -aιl, *g. s.*

foġaιnιm, I serve; -ġnaṁ, *inf.*

foġlamaιm, I learn; -ġluιm, *inf.*

foιġιο, *f.*, patience; -e, *g. s.*

fóιll (ᵹo), hitherto.

foιllsιġιm, I declare; -ιuġaṁ, *inf.*

foιrċιοιοl (-ċeaᵭal), *m.*, doctrine; -ouιl, *g. s.*

foιrleιċeaᵭaċ, extensive; -ouιġe, *comp.*

foláιr, used only in the phrase nι foláιr. It may be translated ' unnecessary ' ; nί foláιn, it is not unnecessary, *i. e.* it is necessary : *cf.* Fr., il faut (O'B., verb ; Coneys, *sub. fem.*, liberty) ; K., fuláιr ; for construction *see* féroιr ; *cf.* faoι lar.

follas, clear.

follasaċ, clear.

foluιġιm, I hide ; folaċ, *inf.*

fonnṁar (ᵹo), cheerfully.

forċóᵹra, *m.*, preface ; —, *g. s.*

foιrleaċan, large ; leιċne, *comp.*

fós, also.

fosᵹlaιm, I open ; -ᵹlaṁ, *inf.*

freaᵹra, *m.*, answer; -ᵹarċa, *g. s.*

froιnsιas, Francis.

fuaᵭaιġιm, I snatch ; fuaᵭaċ, *inf.*

fuasᵹlaιm, I ransom ; -aṁ, *inf.*

fuasᵹuιlċeóιr, *m.*, redeemer; -óra, *g. s.*

fuaċ, *m.*, hatred ; -a, *g. s.*

fuιl, *f.*, blood ; fola, *g. s.*

fuιrιġιm, I wait; fuιreaċ, *inf.*

fulanᵹaιm, I suffer; fulanᵹ, *inf.*

furṁór, *m.*, chief part; -óιr, *g. s.*

E

ᵹᴀḃᴀɪm, I take, pass; -ḃáιl, *inf.*; ᵹᴀḃáιl ᵹo ρeiᵹ ᴀιρ, to pass readily over, connive at.

ᵹᴀċ, each.

ᵹᴀn, without. The only negative that can be used with infin. or gerund : *see* ᴠo. Cf. Fr. ' sans faire.' The Latins do not use *sine* with gerund, though other preps. are frequently employed with it. ' To forgive sins or not to forgive them,' ρeᴀcᴀɪḃe ᴠo ṁᴀιċeᴀḃ no ᵹᴀn ᴀ mᴀιċeᴀḃ.

ᵹᴀoιḃeᴀl, *m.*, Irishman; -ḃιl, *g. s.*

ᵹᴀoιḃeιlᵹ, *f.*, Irish language; -e, *g. s.*

ᵹeᴀllᴀιm, I promise; -leᴀṁuιn, *inf.*

ᵹeᴀll, *m.*, promise; ᵹιll, *g. s.*; mᴀρ ᵹeᴀll ᴀιρ, for the sake of.

ᵹeᴀllᴀṁuιn, *f.*, promise; -ṁnᴀ, *g. s.*

ᵹéᴀɾlonᵹ, *m.*, close investigation; -luιρᵹ, *g. s.*

ᵹeιḃιᴅ, *see* ᴠoᵹeιḃιm.

ᵹéιllιm, I submit; -eᴀḃ, *inf.*

ᵹeιneᴀṁuιn, *f.*, nature; -neᴀṁnᴀ, *g. s.*

ᵹéιnḃɾeᴀċnuιᵹιm, *m.*, I closely consider; -uᵹᴀḃ, *inf.*

ᵹéιɾceᴀᵹᴀᵹᵹ, *m.*, short catechism; -ᴀιρᵹ, *g. s.*

ᵹιḃ, although.

ᵹιḃeᴀḃ, yet.

ᵹlᴀcᴀιm, I receive; -ᴀḃ, *inf.*

ᵹlᴀnᴀιm, I cleanse; -ᴀḃ, *inf.*

ᵹloιne, *f.*, cleanness; —, *g. s.*

ᵹluᴀιsιm, I move; ᵹluᴀρᴀċc, *inf.*

ᵹnáιcċleᴀċcᴀιm, I practise; -ᴀḃ, *inf.*

ᵹnác (ᴠo), continually.

ᵹnácᴀċ, customary.

ᵹné, *f.*, kind; —, *g. s.*

ᵹníoṁ, *m.*, deed, experience; *m.*, -ᴀ, *g. s.*

ᵹnocuιᵹe, *f.*, affair; —, *g. s.*

ᵹo, *prep.*, to (Mid. Ir. *co*).

ᵹo, *prep.*, with (ecl.) (Mid. Ir. *co*, ecl.).

ᵹo, a particle, used for converting adjectives into adverbs.

ᵹo, *conj.* (ecl.), (Mid. Ir. *co*, ecl.), that.

ᵹoιllιm, I am troublesome; -eᴀḃ, *inf.* (followed by ᴀιρ before the person who suffers).

ᵹoιɾιm, I call; -eᴀḃ, *inf.*; acc. of denomination given; dat., with prep. ᴠe, of the thing denominated, v. g. ' The holy Fathers call penance a painful baptism,' ᴠo ᵹoιριᴠ nᴀ h-ᴀιċρeᴀċᴀ nᴀoṁċᴀ bᴀιρᴠeᴀḃ ᴀnᴀcρᴀċ ᴠo'n ᴀιċριᵹe.

ᵹɾáḃ, *m.*, love; —, *g. s.*

ᵹɾáḃuιᵹιm, I love; -uᵹᴀḃ, *inf.*

ᵹɾáιn, *f.*, hatred; ᵹρánnᴀċ, *g. s.*

ᵹɾáιneᴀṁuιl, hateful.

ȝრაosოა, lewd.

ȝრáს, *m.*, grace; and -ა, *g. s.* By D. used in *pl.*, though English equivalent is singular: ოo ȝრáრაიჩ ჩé, on the grace of God.

ȝრeაmuiȝim, I seize, order; -uȝაჩ, *inf.*

ȝრíoსuiȝim, I excite; -uȝაჩ, *inf.*

ȝuიჩim, I pray; ȝuiჩe, *inf.*

ȝuiლim, I weep, deplore; ȝul, *inf.*; ȝoლა, *g. s.*, *m.*

ȝuრ = ȝo რo, used frequently before perfect tense, v.g. ȝuრ ȝლაცაoარ, 'that they received'; not to be confounded with the following.

ȝuრ = ȝuრჩ, enclitic form pres. of iჵ: *see* აცáim.

iარ, *prep.* (ecl.), after; generally written here აiრ. Used by D. and all good writers to express the English *past. part. pass.* Construction is *prep.*, *poss. pr.*, *infin.*: Church assembled, eაȝluiჵ აiრ ჵა coiṁცioჵól; understanding blinded, ცuiȝრe აiრ ჵა oალლაჩ. This prep. iარ has given rise to the the Anglo-Irishism, 'He is after killing him,' meaning, he has killed him.

iარȝჵó, *f.*, grief; —, *g. s.*

iარრაim, I ask; iარრაიჩ, *inf.*

imცiȝim, I depart; imცeაცც, *inf.*

iჵცრeioცe, fit to be believed.

iჵoéuჵცა, fit to be done, filled.

iჵiარრცა, that may be fairly demanded.

iჵṁeაჩóჵაც, interior.

ioცჵლáiჵცeაც, wholesome.

iomაoაṁuiლ, multitudinous.

iomარცაიჩ, *f.*, overmuch; -ჩe, *g. s.*

iomცuჩაიჩ, suitable.

ioმჩა, many.

ioმლáჵ, *m.*, whole; -áiჵ, *g. s.*

ioმჩoუṁლაცც, *f.*, multitude; -ა, *g. s.*

ioჵá, than.

ioჵაჩ, *m.*, place.

ioჵṁúiჵცe, teachable.

ioჵṁuiჵ, dear.

ioჵჵ, in.

ioჵჵაჵ, same.

ioჵჵას, in order (that).

ioჵჵსაჵ, *see prep.* ა.

íoსა, Jesus.

ioსeჩ, Joseph.

iს, assertive verb: *see* აცáim.

iს აჵ = i რiჵ, Mid. Ir.; = რაჵ, Mod. Ir., in the.

ıⲧıⲟⳘⲣáıóⲧⲉⲁ̇ⲥ, given to slander.
ıⳙⳅⲁıⲅ̇ⲉ, *m.*, Jew ; —, *g. s.*
ıⳙⲇⲁⲋ, Judas.

Lⲁ̇ⲃⲣⲁıⳘ, I speak ; Lⲁⲃⲁıⲣⲉ, *pf.*
Lⲁⲉⲧⲉⲁ̇Ⳙⳙıⳑ, daily.
Lⲁ́ıⳘ ⲣⲉ́, beside.
Lⲁ́Ⳙⲁⲥⲁ́ⲛ, *m.*, creeping on all fours ; -ⲁıⲛ, *g. s.*
Lⲁ́Ⳙ, *f.*, hand ; Lⲁ́ıⳘⲉ, *g. s.*
Lⲁ́ⲛⲋⳙⳑ, *m.*, fulness, with reference to the eye.
Lⲉ́, *prep.*, with, by ; Mid. Ir. Lⲁ, Lⲉ ; and govg. acc. and dat.; here at least once
      govs. acc. : Lⲉ ⲥⲟⲣⲣ ⲫⲟⲥⲁıⳑ. In mod. writers, dat., Lⲉ́ ⲁ, by which ; Lⲉⲟ́,
      with them.
Lⲉⲁⲃⲁⲣ, *m.*, book ; -ⲁıⲣ, *g. s.*
Lⲉⲁⲃⲣⲁ́ⲛ, *m.*, little book ; -ⲁıⲛ, *g. s.*
Lⲉⲁⲃⲣⲁ́ⲛⳙⲣⲛⲁıⲅ̇ⲧⲉ, *m.*, prayerbook.
Lⲉⲁⲛⲁⲃ̇, *m.*, child ; Lⲉıⲛⲃ̇, *g. s.*
Lⲉⲁⲋⳙıⲅ̇ıⳘ, I amend ; -ⳙⲅ̇ⲁⲃ̇, *inf.*
Lⲉⲁⲧ, *f.*, half, side ; Lⲉıⲥ̇ⲉ, *g. s.*
Lⲉⲁⲧⲁⳅⲁ̇ⲥ, wide, extensive.
LⲉⲁⲧⲁⳘⳙıⲅ̇, except (followed by ⳅⲟ).
Lⲉⲁⲧⲛⳙıⲅ̇ıⳘ, I spread ; -ⳙⲅ̇ⲁⲃ̇, *inf.*
LⲉⲁⲧⲧⲣⲟⳘ, *m.*, affliction ; -ⲧⲣⳙıⳘ, *g. s.*
LⲉⲁⲧⲧⲣⲟⳘⲁ̇ⲥ, afflicted.
Lⲉ́ıⲅ̇ıⳘ, I read ; -ⲅ̇ⲉⲁⲃ̇, *inf.*
Lⲉ́ıⲅıⳘ, I leave ; Lⲉ́ıⲅıⲟⲛ, *inf.*
Lⲉ́ıⲅıⲟⲛⲛ, *m.*, lesson, literature ; -ıⲛⲛ, *g. s.*
Lⲉ́ıⲅ̇ⲉⲁⲋ, *m.*, cure ; -ⲅ̇ıⲣ, *g. s.*
Lⲉ́ıⲣ, clear.
Lⲉ́ıⲣ (ⲅⲟ), altogether.
Lⲉıⲋⲅ̇ⲉ, *f.*, sloth ; —, *g. s.*
Lⲉıⲧⲉⲁⳅ, *m.*, breadth ; -ıⳅ, *g. s.*
Lⲉıⲧⲉⲁⳅⲁ̇ⲥ, extensive.
Lⲉıⲧⲋⲅ̇ⲉⲁⳑ, *m.*, excuse ; -ⲉ́ıⳑ, *g. s.*
Lⲉⲟ́ⲣ, enough.
Lⲉⲟıⲣⲅ̇ⲛⲓⲟⳘ, *m.*, satisfaction ; -ⲁ, *g. s.*
LⲓⲟⲛⲁıⳘ, I fill ; -ⲁⲃ̇, *inf.*
LⲓⲟⲛⳘⲁⲣ, abundant.
Lⲟ́, *m.*, day ; Lⲁⲟı, *g. s.* ; Lⲟ́, *d. s.*
Lⲟⲃⲁⲛ, Louvain.
Lⲟⲥⲧ, *f.*, fault ; -ⲁ, *g. s.*
Lⲟⲥⲧⲁ̇ⲥ, sinful.

loιτim, I wound; loτ, *inf.*
lomnoττ, naked.
lonᵹ, *m.*, track; luinᵹ, *g. s.*
luaċ, *m.*, price; luaιᵹ, *g. s.*
luττ, *m.*, people; —, *g. s.*
luᵹa, less.
luιᵹim, I lie; luιᵹe, *inf.*; luιᵹe arτeaċ aιn, encroachment on.

mac, *m.*, son; mιc, *g. s.*
macaoṁ, *m.*, a youth; -oιṁ, *g. s.*; -a poᵹlumτa, learned folk.
máḃ, if; *see also* aτáιm.
maḋraḃ, *m.*, dog; -aιḃ, *g. s.*
maιḋιn, *f.*, morning; -ḋne, *g. s.*
maιlle ṅé, together with.
maιτ, good.
maιτeaċ, forgiven.
maιτim, I forgive; -eaḃ, *inf.*
maιτeaṁnas, *m.*, forgiveness; -uιr, *g. s.*
maιτeas, *m.*, goodness; -a, *g. s.*
maιτreaċ, forgiven.
malluιᵹim, I curse; -uᵹaḃ, *inf.*
manéur, *m.*, manor; -éιr, *g. s.*
maoιḃim, I boast; maoιḃeaṁ, *inf.*
maoιḋreaċus, *m.*, boasting; -uιr, *g. s.*
maoιn, *f.*, wealth; -e, *g. s.*
maoτ, tender; maoιτe, *g. s.,f.*
man, *prep. and conj.*, as.
maraon ṅé, together with.
marḃaim, I kill; -aḃ, *inf.*; -marḃτa, *g. s.*; peacaḃ marḃτa, mortal sin.
masluιᵹim, I dishonour; -uᵹaḃ, *inf.*
máτaιr, *f.*, mother; -ar, *g. s.*
meaḃaιr, *f.*, memory.
méaḋuιᵹim, I increase; -uᵹaḃ, *inf.*
meallaιm, I deceive; -llaḃ, *inf.*
mearḃall, *m.*, error; -aιll, *g. s.*
measᵹ (a), amidst.
measuim, I think, esteem; mear, *inf.*
meιnιc (ᵹo), frequently.
mιan, *m. and f.*, desire; -a, méιne, *g. s.*
mιanᵹus, *m.*, inordinate desire; -uιr, *g. s.*
mιċáel, Michael; -ċíl, *g. s.*

míġníoṁ, *m.*, bad deed; -ᴀ, *g. s.*

milliṁ, I destroy; -eᴀḃ, *inf.*

millτeᴀċ, destructive.

míle, a thousand; —, *g. s.*; mílτe, *n. p.*

minic; *see* meinic.

míniġim, I explain; -iuġᴀᴅ, *inf.*; -ġċe, *g. s.*, explanation.

míocᴀrτᴀnᴀċ, uncharitable.

míoċlú, *f.*, bad fame; —, *g. s.*

míoċoṁġᴀr, *m.*, inconvenience; -ᴀ¹ɼ, *g. s.*

mioḃúτċusᴀċ, degenerate.

míonᴀireᴀċ, shameless.

mionċuᴀrτuiġim, I closely examine; -uġᴀḃ, *inf.*

mionnuiġim, I swear; -uġᴀḃ, *inf.*

mionrᴀnn, *m.*, small district; -ᴀ, *g. s.*

mionsᴀoτᴀr, *m.*, small work; -ᴀ¹ɼ, *g. s.*

mionτosᴀċ, *m.*, small beginning; -ui₃, *g. s.*; in *pl.*, elements.

míorḃuil, *f.*, miracle; -e, *g. s.*

misneᴀċ, *m. and f.*, courage, encouragement; -niġe, *g. s.*

moċ, early.

mór, great.

mórᴀn, *m.*, much, many; -áin, *g. s.*

mórġᴀnτᴀnus, *m.*, great scarcity; -uiɼ, *g. s.*

mórluᴀiġ, precious.

mórṁór (ᴣo), chiefly.

mórolc, *m.*, great evil; -uilc.

muc, *f.*, pig; *pl.*, swine, muice, *g. s.*

muiniġin, *f.*, confidence; -e, *g. s.*

muiriġin, *f.*, burthen; -e, *g. s.*

muinτir, *f.*, family, people; -e, *g. s.*

muinτirḃeᴀs, *m.*, friendship, kindness; -iɼ, *g. s.*

múinim, I teach; múnᴀḃ, *inf.*

munᴀ, unless; *see* ᴀτáim.

n' *for* nᴀ.

nᴀ, a part of pronom. comp. ɼenᴀ: *see* ɼé.

ná, nor.

nᴀċ, not (in clauses dependent).

nᴀċ ᴀr, = nᴀċᴀɼ, = náɼ, forms which nᴀċ takes when combined with the prefix ɼo.

nᴀċ ᴀr, in construction, nᴀċ ᴀɼ ḃɼéiᴅiɼ: *see* ᴀτáim.

nᴀṁᴀᴅᴀs, *m.*, enmity; -uiɼ, *g. s.*

nᴀṁuiᴅ, *m.*, enemy; -ṁᴀᴅ, *g. s.*

naoimċéile, *f.*, holy spouse; —, *g. s.*

naoṁ, holy.

naoṁaim, I sanctify; -aḃ, *inf.*

náṛ, *see* naċ aṛ.

naṛ, abbreviation for ı n-aṛ, 'in our'; naṛ n-oıaıḃ, in our sequence, which follows. Cf. *H.*, line 64, ı n-aṛ noıaıḃ, 'in the sequel.'

neaċ, one, anyone.

neaṁċráḃaḋ, *m.*, impiety; -aıḃ, *g. s.*

neaṁṫa, heavenly.

neaṛt, *m.*, strength; néıṛt, *g. s.*

neaṛtṁaṛ, strong.

neıṁċıontaċ, innocent; -uıże, *comp.*

ní, not (in independent clauses).

ní, is not; *see* atáım.

ní, *m.*, thing; neıċe, *g. s.*

ní, 3rd *sg. pres.*; *see* ḋoním.

níos, *sign of comp.*

no, or

noċ, he who, they who, &c.; Lat. *is qui.*

no żo, until.]

noıs, (a), now.

nós, *m.*, manner; nóıṛ, *g. s.*

nuaḋḋúıl, *f.*, new creature; -ḋúılle, *g. s.*

nuaıḋḃeata, *f.*, new life; —, *g. s.*

nuaıútıonszantóıṛ, *m.*, new beginner; -óṛa, *g. s.*

nuıże, żo —— so, up to this.

ó, *prep.*, from; uaċa, from them; uaḃ, from him; ó, from which; ó'ṛ *for* ó ıṛ; ó ṛın ṛuaṛ, for the future; ó tá, since.

oḃaıṛ, *f.*, work; oıḃṛe, *g. s.*

óż, young.

oıḃṛıżım, I compose; -ıużaḋ, *inf.*

oıḋċe, *f.*, night; —, *g. s.*

oıḋe, *m.*, instructor; —, *g. s.*

oıḋeas, *m.*, instruction; ıṛ, *g. s.*

óıże, *f.*, youth; —, *g. s.*

oılḃéımeaċ, scandalous.

oıle, other.

óıṛ, for, because.

oıṛḋeıṛc, illustrious.

óıṛeaċous, *m.*, assembly; -uıṛ, *g. s.*

oıṛeaṁnaċ, fitting.

oıreaṁuın, *f.*, fitness.
oıríseal, humble.
ólacán, *m.*, drinking.
olc, *m.*, evil; oılc, *g. s.*
ollas, *m.*, pomp.
ollṁuıᵹım, I prepare; -uᵹaḋ, *inf.*
orᴅ, *m.*, order; uırᴅ, oırᴅ, *g. s.*
orᴅuıᵹım, I order; -uᵹaḋ, *inf.*
ós aırᴅ, openly.
ós cıonn, *prep.*, over.

páᵹánaċ, *m.*, Pagan; -uıᵹ, *g. s.*
páıpéur, *m.*, paper; éır, *g. s.*
peacaċ, *m.*, sinner; -aıᵹ, *g. s.*
peacaḋ, *m.*, sin; -aıḋ, *g. s.*
pıan, *f.*, pain; péıne, *g. s.*
pılıp, Philip.
popul, *m.*, people; -uıl, *g. s.*
préaṁ, *f.*, root; préıṁe, *g. s.*

raḋaıᴅ, *see* atáım.
racaıḋ, *see* teıḃım.
ráḋ, *see* aᴅeırım.
rann, *m.*, part; -nna, *g. s.*
rannpáırteaċ, participating.
ré, *prep.*, with, towards; Mid. Irish, *fri*, governing acc. and dat. Now governs dat., though here found with acc. ré ᴄurcuıᵹ. With art. rır an; rır, with him; rıu, with them; ré a, ré ar, ré, with which; ré na, with his. O'D. does not correctly explain the existence of n here, which he ascribes to euphony. Better, perhaps, written rena, according to analogy with other pronominal compounds; re h-aᵹaıḋ, 'for the benefit of.'
réıᵹ, ready; léıᵹıon ᴄorċa ᵹo, to pass readily over, to connive at.
réım, *f.*, aim, extent; -e, *g. s.*
reuṁráıᴅᴄe, aforesaid.
nıaċᴄanaċ, necessary.
nıaċᴄanus, *m.*, necessity; -uır, *g. s.*
rıaṁ (a), ever.
rıaraım, I serve; rıar, -aḋ, *inf.*
rıoıre, *m.*, knight; —, *g. s.*
rınneaḋ, *see* ᴅoním.
ríoᵹa, royal.
ríoᵹaċᴄ, *f.*, kingdom; -a, *g. s.*

Riotaim, I run; riot, *inf.*
Rírib (ba), really.
Ro, too.
Ro, verbal particle before past tense, found now in *comp.*; v. g. nár.
Roga, *f.*, choice; -an, *g. s.*; -uin, *d. s.*
Roim, *prep.*, before; Mid. Irish, re, ria (ecl.), rompa, before them.
Roinn, *f.*, portion; -nne, *g. s.*
Roinnim, I divide; roinn. *inf.*
Ruatar, *m.*, act of rushing; -air, *g. s.*
Rugab, *see* beirim.
Rúinbiamair, *f.*, mystery.
Rún, *m.*, resolution; rúin, *g. s.*

Sa, for ir an, which see.
Sa, *see* ro.
Sacramuint, *f.*, sacrament; -e, *g. s.*
Sáirmeasamuil, very estimable.
Sáitim, I thrust, plunge; satab, *inf.*
Samuil, like.
San, emph. affix to pronouns; v. g. bóib-ran.
Sanasán, *m.*, decision; -áin, *g. s.*
Saobnós, *m.*, foolish habit; -óir, *g. s.*
Saogal, *m.*, world, life; -uil, *g. s.*
Saogalta, worldly.
Saoilim, I think; saoilrin, *inf.*
Saoirse, *f.*, freedom; —, *g. s.*
Saoraim, I deliver; -ab, *inf.*
Saotar, *m.*, labour; -air, *g. s.*
Saotrac, laborious.
Sársaotar, hard labour.
Sáruigim, I surpass, transgress; -ugab, *inf.*
Sásam, *m.*, satisfaction.
Sásuigim, I satisfy; sárab, sáram, *inf.*
Se, *see* ro.
Sé, *pers. pr.*, he, it; rí, she, it; riab, *pl.*; e, him; i, her (*acc.*); iab, them. With ir and pass. verbs, nom. case, é, he; í, she; iab, *pl.* With the verb ir its use is proleptic in such phrases as ir é an bár an marcac úb, 'Death is that horseman;' ir í an íomaig úb an nabúir baonna, 'that image is human nature,' and the proof that that is so is that it must take the gender of the subject (see the discussion in Appendix to Keating, Trí b—g an báir, p. i.). Thus, in English, we say, 'to err is human;' but with prolepsis, 'it is human to err.' Cobbet condemns this proleptical use of 'it' in English, but usage is against him.

seaċnaim, I avoid ; -aḋ, ṗeaċain, ṗeaċainc, *inf.*

seaċc (*ecl.*), seven.

seal, *m.*, time ; -a, *g. s.*

seanṗalcanaċ, inveterately hostile.

seanmóiṙ, *f.*, sermon ; -óṙa, *g. s.*

seanḃṗóġancuiḋe, *m.*, servant ; —, *g. s.*

seiṁ, soft, indulgent.

sġaṗaim, I scatter ; -aḋ, *inf.*

sġaṙaim, I separate ; -aḋ, -aṁuin, *inf.*

sġéiṁ, *f.*, beauty ; -e, *g. s.*

sġeicim, I omit ; ṛġeiḃ, *inf.*

sġeac, *f.*, shield ; ṛġeiċe.

sġṙíḃinn, *f.*, Scripture ; -e, *g. s.*

sġṙíoḃaim, I write ; -aḋ, *inf.*

sġṙiosaim, destroy ; ṛġṙios, *inf.*

sġuiṙim, I cease ; ṛġuṙ, *inf.*

sí, *see* ṛe.

si, suffix to 2*nd pers. pl.*

sin, *dem. pr.*, that (indecl.). In nom. and acc. relation can stand alone for a subst., and be subject or object in a sentence. In dat. it occasionally is governed directly by prep., but usually it requires the intervention of pers. pronoun, uime ṛin, therefore, where uime = um é. In genitive relation always takes poss. pr. a, oṛ a ċionn ṛin, ṿa ċaob ṛin. As to the separation between a and ṛin, *see* def. article an.

Dem. pronom. adj. ṛin, and by vowel harmony ṛoin—an element in the dem. pronom. adj. an . . . ṛin.

Adverb—an element in the correlative adverb coṁ — ṛin, with relative conjunction aġuṛ.

    Coiṁṿiomḃuiḋeaċ ṛin aġuṛ cṛoiḋ, 'so ungrateful as to fight.'

    Coṁṿána ṛin aġuṛ ceampoll Ḋé ṿo ċṛuailluġaḋ, 'so bold as to defile the temple of God.'

    Cf. the Anglo-Irishism, 'He was *that* glad that he leaped for joy,' &c. This idea would be expressed in English (if the phrase were admissible), ' He was that*ly* glad that he leaped for joy.'

    As to separation between coṁ and ṛin in these phrases *see* def. article.

siocaiṙ, *f.*, occasion ; -cṛaċ, *g. s.*

síoṙṙuiḋe, lasting.

síos, below.

síṙim, I seek ; -eaḋ, *inf.*

siúḃlaim, I walk, depart ; -ḃal, *inf.* ; ṗuaṿaiġim aiṙ ṛúḃal, I snatch away.

slaṿaim, I plunder ; -ṛlaṿ, *inf.*

sláince, *f.*, health ; —, *g. s.*

slánuiġim, I save ; -uġaḋ, *inf.*

slánuiġceóiṙ, *m.*, Saviour ; -óṙa, *g. s.*

slige, *f.*, way; —, *g. s.*

sluigim, I swallow; slugaḋ, *inf.*

smaċtuigim, I correct; -uġaḋ, *inf.*

smuainim, I think, meditate; -eaḋ, *inf.*

so, *dem. pr.*, this; indecl., but following in case relation the same laws as rin, which see.

    Dem. pronom. adj., an element in the dem. pronom. adj., an . . . ro, v. g.; an teaġarg ro, this doctrine. It also appears in this last construction under the forms ra, re, rı.

soċar, *m.*, advantage; -air, *g. s.*

soilléir, quite clear.

soillsigim, I enlighten; -uġaḋ, *inf.*

so mar, thus.

son (air), for the sake of; governs gen.

sotuigseaċ, easily understood; -ġte, *comp.*

sotuigsionaċ, intelligible.

spioraḋ, *m.*, spirit; -aiṿ, *g. s.*

spioraḋalta, spiritual.

srian, *m.*, bridle; -ain, *g. s.*

suas, up, above.

suḃáilce, *f.*, virtue; —, *g. s.*

suiġiġim, I place; -iuġaḋ.

súil, *f.*, eye; -e, *g. s.*

suil, before.

súnraḋaċ, special.

tá, *see* atáim.

taḃairt, *see* voḃeirim.

táinig, *see* tigim.

tairḃe, *f.*, profit; —, *g. s.*

taisbeánaiṁ, I show; -aḋ, *inf.* (differently accented elsewhere, but pronounced as written here).

taitiġim, I frequent; taitiġe, *inf.*

talmuiġe, earthly.

tan, *f.*, time; an tan, when.

taoḃ, *f.*, side; taoiḃe, *g. s.*; taoḃ aroiġ, inwardly; vo taoḃ, with respect to.

tar, *prep.*, beyond; tort, beyond thee; torta, beyond them; vul tort, to pass away; tar éir; after (with gen.); tar ċeann, notwithstanding; tar ċionn, besides.

tarcuisne, *f.*, disrespect; -e, *g. s.*

tarcuisniġim, I dishonour; -iuġaḋ, *inf.*

tarruinġim, I draw; tarruinġ, *inf.*

teaġarg, *m.*, teaching, catechism; -airg, *g. s.*

ceaᵹṁaim, I meet with (followed by ne; ceiᵹṁeoᵹuiꝺ, 3rd pl. fut. (followed by ꝺo), happen to : ma ceaᵹṁann ꝺo'n cuiꝺ ꝺóib, 'if it happens to some of them.'

ceanᵹa, f., tongue; -aꝺ, g. s.

céiꝺim, I go; ċuaiꝺ, 3 s. perf.; -ꝺul, inf.

ceilᵹim, I cast; ceilᵹion, ceilᵹean, inf.

ceipim, I fail.

ceisbeánaꝺ, m., show.

ceiċim, I flee; ceiċeaṁ, inf.

ciᵹeanna, m., lord; —, g. s.

ciᵹim, I come; ceaċc, inf.; ciᵹear, pres. rel.; cáiniᵹ, 3rd sg. perf.; ciacfaꝺ, 3rd s. cond.; ᵹo ꝺ-ciᵹ leoran, that they can.

cimċillᵹeánraim, I circumcise; -aꝺ, inf.

cimċioll, about.

cioꝺlaice, m., gift.

ciomáinaim, I drive; ciomáin, inf.

ciomsuiᵹim, I collect; -uᵹaꝺ, inf.

ciomsuiᵹceóir, m., collector; -óna, g. s.

cionsᵹainim, I begin; -ᵹnaꝺ, inf.

cionsᵹancóir, m., beginner; -óna, g. s.

cín, f., country; -e, g. s.

cnuc, m., envy; -uiċ, g. s.

cobar, m., fountain; -air, g. s.

coᵹaim, I choose; -ᵹaꝺ, inf.; -ċa, pass. part.

coil, f., will; cola, coile, g. s.

coilceanaċ, willing.

coirmeasᵹ, m., hindrance; -mirᵹ, g. s.

coirc, f., bulk; -e, g. s.

coraꝺ, m., fruit; -aiꝺ, g. s.

cosuiᵹim, I begin; -uᵹaꝺ, inf.

cosaċ, m., beginning; -uiᵹ, g. s.

cnácaṁuil, timely.

cnácnóna, m., evening; —, g. s.

cné, prep., through; Mid. Ir. tria, tre, with acc. and dat.; now usually with dat.; but here once with acc.: cné ċionca; with art., cner an; 3rd s. pers. pr., cniꝺ; with rel., cné, cné a, cné an.

cnéiᵹim, I forsake; -ᵹion, inf.

cnenc, Trent.

cníoċaꝺ, thirty.

cnócaire, f., mercy; —, g. s.

cnócaireaċ, merciful.

cnoiꝺim, I fight; cnoiꝺ, inf.

cnosᵹaꝺ, m., fasting; -aiꝺ, g. s.

cruaiġe, *f.*, pity ; —, *g. s.*

cruaillim, I corrupt ; -eaḋ, *inf.* ; -uġaḋ.

cuairim, *f.*, drift ; ɼ'an cuaiɼim ɼin, thereabouts.

cuacaṁail, vulgar.

cubaisceaċ, mischievous ; -iġ, *g. s.*

cuġ, *see* ꝺoḃeiɼim.

cuiġim, I understand ; cuiġɼin, *inf.*

cuiġse, *f.*, understanding ; —, *g. s.*

cuiġsionaċ, intelligence.

cuile, *f.*, flood ; —, *g. s.*

cuilleaḋ, *m.*, addition, more.

cuismiġim, I bring forth ; -meaḋ, *inf.*

cuismiġceóir, *m.*, parent ; -óɼa, *g. s.*

cuicim, I fall ; —, *inf.*

curcaċ, *m.*, Turk ; -uiġ, *acc. pl.*

cús, *m.*, beginning ; cúiɼ, *g. s.*

uaḃar, *m.*, pride ; -aiɼ, *g. s.*

uaiḃreaċ, proud.

uaiġneaċ, secret ; -uiġe, *g. s.*, *f.*

uair, *f.*, hour ; -e, *g. s.* ; uair ɼa m-bliaḋain, once a-year ; aon uair aṁain, once ; aiɼ uairiḃ, sometimes.

uasal, precious, noble ; uaiɼle, *n. p.*, *f.*

ualaċ, *m.*, obligation ; -aiġ, *g. s.*

uacḃásaċ, dreadful.

uċ, oh! alas!

úꝺ, yonder ; an element in the *dem. pronom. adj.*, 'that': *see* ɼin.

uġꝺarás, *m.*, authority ; -aiɼ.

uile, all.

uireasḃaiḋ, *f.*, want ; -ḃe, *g. s.*

uisġe, *m.*, water ; —, *g. s.*

ullaṁ, ready.

ullṁuiġim, I prepare ; -uġaḋ, *inf.*

uim, about, around ; uime, about him ; iompa, about them.

uras, easy.

urcóiꝺ, *f.*, wickedness ; -e, *g. s.*

urcóiꝺeaċ, wicked.

urnaiġ, *f.*, prayer ; -aiġce, *n. p.*

urraim, *f.*, reverence ; -e, *g. s.*

ursa, *f.*, pillar ; -nn, *g. s.*

Printed by Ponsonby & Weldrick, Dublin.

www.ingramcontent.com/pod-product-compliance
Lightning Source LLC
Chambersburg PA
CBHW032044090426
42733CB00030B/654